2E2

John Hedgecoe's

THE ART OF
COLOUR
PHOTOGRAPHY

John Hedgecoe's

THE ART OF
COLOUR
PHOTOGRAPHY

MITCHELL BEAZLEY

**John Hedgecoe's
The Art of Colour Photography**

This new edition first published in Great Britain in
1998 by Mitchell Beazley,
an imprint of Reed Consumer Books Limited
Michelin House, 81 Fulham Road
London SW3 6RB and Auckland

All photographs by John Hedgecoe
Assistant **Jenny Mackintosh**

Contributing editor **Jonathan Hilton**

Executive art editor **Janis Utton**
Executive editor **Judith More**
Project art editor **Susan Downing**
Layout designer **Tony Spalding**
Production controller **Rachel Staveley**
Indexer **Ann Parry**

A CIP catalog record for this book is available
from the British Library

ISBN 1 84000 044 9

Set in Frutiger
Produced by Toppan Printing Company Limited
Printed in China

Contents

Introduction

Photography is the most accessible of all art forms. It is a medium open to everybody, yet there is a profound difference between a good photographer and somebody who simply aims a camera at the world and trips the shutter. The difference is a matter partly of technical knowledge and partly of intuition, imagination, and trained perception. The aim of this book is not to display photographs and make artistic claims for them; it is to encourage you to develop your own skill and insight and to make you more aware of the creative choices that are involved every time you take a picture. As you make these choices you may discover that what began as a pastime has become an art.

Until relatively recently, the photographs many people regarded as "art" were black and white abstractions of reality. This attitude was a result both of an historical accident and of a misunderstanding of what is unique about the photographic image. The reason why the pioneers of photography made black and white pictures was that they lacked the technical means to make color ones. Potentially, color was always a vital ingredient, but color film stock did not become readily available until the late 1930s.

Although intuitively we respond more readily to colors than to shapes, we tend to think of color in stereotypical ways – foliage being green in

◁ **A touch of color,** if used in the correct proportion, need not monopolize attention by dominating the composition. To achieve this result, I waited for a shaft of sunlight to highlight the boat and wheeling gulls against the shadow area of the towering cliffs behind, but their relatively small scale leaves the eye free to explore the detail contained within the entire frame.

◁ **Regular rows of lavender** – the color of their flower heads changing depending on how the light strikes them – lead the eye deep into the photograph. The low shooting angle and generous depth of field of a wide-angle lens exaggerate the front-to-back perspective of the shot to create a compelling and detailed landscape scene.

△ **The careful placement** of an element of known size – the human figure – lends an immediate sense of scale to this color-rich agricultural scene. Although taking up only a tiny part of the overall picture area, its near-central placement in an opening in the lush foliage imparts greater importance than size alone would indicate.

summer and brown in autumn, for example. The first step in understanding color is the realization that everything in the world changes its hue according to the quality of the light by which we view it. Colors may appear unnatural, but no color can really be called true or untrue.

The elements that go into making a successful color photograph are explained in detail in this book. In addition to tone, hue, form, pattern, line, texture, and shape – the basic compositional elements of most graphic arts – they include the special and often subtle relationships between different colors. The way in which colors are affected by different backgrounds, and the overriding importance of the angle of view in relation to the changing light, are also fundamental aspects of color photography. But when these lessons have been absorbed it is still your individual response to a scene or subject that will determine whether or not you take a successful picture. For a successful photograph depends on a series of personal choices the photographer has

△ **Camera and subject movement** have both had an effect on this action-filled composition. Selecting a slow shutter speed in the overcast lighting, I panned the camera as the skier flashed past to keep him in roughly center frame throughout the exposure. All static parts of the scene were, thus, reduced to little more than an abstract blur.

▷ **Subdued studio lighting,** coming from a tungsten spotlight positioned in front of the subject, so that its lighting head shone slightly down on her face, has produced an essentially monochromatic image. The softness of the image and the intriguing highlights on the lips were brought about by subject movement during the exposure.

▷ **The form and texture** of wrinkled apples have been emphasized by the dominance of their yellow, red, and brown hues against a subdued background, which contains muted echoes of the same colors. A brighter background may well have fought for interest and destroyed the impact of the picture.

made about it – about the elements included, the range of tones, the mood, and, above all, the decisive moment at which to press the shutter and expose the film.

You also need to take account of the new, affordable, and increasingly accessible innovations now available, which have been brought about as a result of digital-imaging techniques and computer manipulation. Although it is now true that the photographic original – be it a positive slide image or a negative – need only be the starting point rather than the end product of the photographic process, the essential components that make a particular image extend beyond the frame, to live and to last, to engage our emotions, and challenge our preconceptions are as important to photography as they ever were.

John Hedgecoe

◁ **You need to rise before dawn** if you want to record images such as this. I photographed this dew-hung spider's web in the gentle light of early morning, when the sun was sufficiently above the horizon to fill the shadows but before it had warmed the atmosphere enough to evaporate those tiny, short-lived droplets of moisture.

△ **The ability to "see" the potential** within the commonplace is one of the key requirements of successful photography. Although the subject matter is prosaic, reflected sidelighting has produced a strongly three-dimensional abstract design that engages the eye and holds your attention, inviting you to explore the shapes and textures of a small panel of peeling paintwork.

What is color?

The colors of light

In 1666 Isaac Newton, then 23 years old, became fascinated by the behavior of sunlight passing through a prism – a glass block of triangular cross-section. His studies led to the realization that color arises from the interaction of light with matter. Each ray of light was refracted by the prism – in other words, it emerged traveling in a different direction from that in which it entered. But not only was the sunlight bent by the prism, it also emerged as a spreading beam of multicolored light, displaying the hues seen in a rainbow, and in the same order. Although there were seven main hues in the spectrum he saw – red, orange, yellow, green, blue, indigo, and violet – these merged into one another.

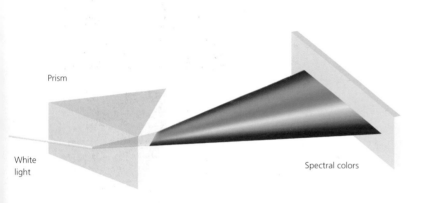

Prism

White light

Spectral colors

◁ **White light,** such as that from sunlight, is analyzed by a prism into a spectrum of colors that ranges from red to violet. Invisible infrared and ultraviolet light extend far beyond the spectrum that the human eye can see.

▽ **White light is reconstituted** when colored light emerging from a prism is recombined by a simple converging lens. The lens of a camera is more complicated than this, however, being made up of an array of lens elements (some converging, some diverging), and each with a different refractive index (ability to bend light). In this way, all the different wavelengths of light can be brought into a common point of focus.

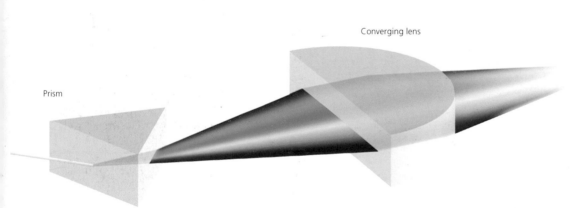

Converging lens

Prism

Reconstituted white light

From his observations of light emerging from a prism, the young Newton concluded that white sunlight was, in fact, a mixture of different types of light, each type being of a single, pure color, and that the prism refracted, or bent, these colors to varying degrees. Red appeared to be refracted the least, violet the most, and the other colors by intermediate amounts. Newton found that when he mixed the colors of a spectrum – for example, by bringing its light to a single point of focus by intro-ducing a lens – he obtained white light once more. Further experimentation involved him in blocking out some colors before recombining the others to obtain colored mixtures of light. Furthermore, the colors he obtained in this way were quite different from any found in the naturally occurring spectrum.

REFLECTION AND ABSORPTION OF LIGHT

What Newton had discovered was that the color of anything in nature depends on the type of light it sends to the eye. This, in turn, depends on both the nature of the light falling on an object and the individual colors in the light that the surface of that object reflects, absorbs, or transmits. If the light falling on a surface lacks some colors, the light reflected back from the surface will also lack those colors. But the "true" color of a reflective surface – the it looks when viewed in a standard white light – can be completely specified by stating in form of a table of numbers, or display-ing as a graph, the proportion of light of each spectral color that it reflects.

If the proportion of reflected colors is similar to the balance found in sunlight (with blue-green predominating and the proportion of the other colors tailing off toward the ends of the spectrum) the surface will appear to be white. But if, for example, there is a greater propor-tion of the colors toward the red end of the spectrum than in sunlight, then the surface will take on a reddish cast; if bluish colors tend to dominate in the reflected light, then the surface will appear to have a blue cast.

The balance of spectral colors that produces particular hues is complex. But it is generally true to say that if a surface looks strongly colored when viewed in white light, it is reflecting certain colors from the light falling on it and strongly absorbing others. If it looks black, it is absorbing all the spectral colors.

LUMINESCENCE
Certain substances not only absorb some of the light energy falling on them but also re-emit it as light of a different color. These substances are called luminescent. The gemstones ruby and spinel, for example, will absorb blue hues in light and emit red.

Ultraviolet light, which is an invisible component of light beyond the violet end of the spectrum, stimulates many substances to emit visible light. If this re-emission ceases immediately when the stimulating light ceases, the effect is called fluorescence. If the glow lingers, it is called phosphorescence.

The extra brightness brought about by some washing powders is achieved by a fluorescent component that is retained in the clothes and is stimulated by the ultraviolet part of sunlight. The extra light that is emitted is sufficient to make the clothes noticeably brighter. Fluorescent poster paints are also stimulated by the ultraviolet component contained in sunlight.

INFRARED LIGHT
Light that is absorbed by a material is converted into heat energy. In 1800 the English astronomer William Herschel discovered an invisible component of sunlight by its warming effect on the bulb of a thermometer. It lay beyond the red end of the spectrum, so he named it "infrared" (meaning "below the red") light. Specialized film will respond to this light, although some focusing correction is required, since this form of light energy does not come into focus at the same point as visible light. As a result, some lenses have an infrared focusing mark engraved on their barrels.

TRANSMITTED LIGHT
Another form of color perception comes from light that is transmitted by transparent substances. You might think it surprising that, say, a portion of a color transparency looks the same color when viewed by reflected light as it does when viewed by the light it transmits (when, for example, seen as a projected image on a screen). Why does it not reflect and absorb some combination of colors and transmit the remainder? The answer is that the light by which we view a transparency, from whichever direction, has been both reflected and transmitted. Light passing through the dye contained in the film emulsion is reflected from millions upon millions pigment particles suspended in a clear medium of gelatin. The light may emerge in any direction from the film and, thus, the film image looks the same color from any angle.

COLOR CORRECTION FOR LENSES
When dealing with certain very thin films, the type of behaviour of reflected and transmitted lighted described above does not hold true. A film of this kind is the microscopically thin anti-reflection coatings used on the glass surfaces of photographic lenses. This coating can minimize reflection only for a narrow range of spectral colors, determined by the thickness of the coating. The color wavelength chosen is in the central regions of the spectrum. Hence, the light reflected from the coating is poor in yellow or green, and the color of the visible "bloom" you can see when you hold a lens up to the light is that obtained when yellow or green is subtracted from white – namely purple.

COLOR DIFFRACTION
Any reflective surface that is engraved with a series of extremely fine lines will cause light falling on it be become fragmented, or diffracted. The colors reflected back will depend on the fineness of the engraving, or the number of lines per square inch, and the angle at which the surface is viewed. Change your angle of view, even slightly, and the colors can shift dramatically from, say, red, orange, or yellow to green, blue, or violet.

In photography, color diffraction is most often used to create a range of bizarre, image-distorting effects. This done by placing a specially engraved clear-glass filter over the camera lens.

RAINBOW HUES

The most common phenomena of the daylight sky – a rainbow – gives us the strongest indication of the true composition of "white" sunlight. A rainbow forms when falling raindrops are illuminated by sunlight. In effect, each drop of moisture becomes a tiny prism, refracting and dispersing light rays before they emerge from the area of rainfall. The intensity of the color of the bow is dependent on the size of the raindrops – when drops are large, violet and green are distinct and blue is largely absent. The colors of a primary rainbow always appear in the same order, since the raindrops that are highest in the sky transmit red light to the observer, while violet light is transmitted by the lowest drops.

The effect, seen most clearly with a high-contrast subject, such a night-time scene containing brightly lit windows in otherwise dark surroundings, will show a string of multicolored images formed from each point of light in the subject. Each of these, apart from the main image, is spread into its components. The exact form of these images will depend on the way the filter is engraved, and in photography the lines are nearly always parallel. You can, however, rotate the filter to change their position in the frame and the colors produced. You can sometimes achieve a similar effect to a diffraction filter by shooting through any partly opaque material.

Color balance

Invisible radiation, from X-rays to radio waves, flanks the narrow spectrum of electromagnetic radiation that is visible as colors to our unaided eye. The human eye is quite limited in its sensitivity, being able to perceive wavelengths that fall only between 0.4 and 0.7 of a micrometer (also known as a micron) – this is the range of light that can be seen as the colors between violet and red. There is some ultraviolet light present in daylight, especially in sky light, and this we see as the atmospheric haze that makes distant hills and mountains appear light-toned in black and white photographs and blue in color ones.

The light by which we view the world around us is known as electromagnetic radiation. Visible light is generated in the outermost regions of atoms that have been heated. Every atom consists of a cloud of electrons orbiting a central nucleus and the number of electrons in each orbit is limited. When a material is heated, its atoms vibrate faster and faster and start to jostle each other more violently, so that some atoms jump to higher-energy orbits, absorbing heat energy as they do so. Later, they fall back into the vacancies created in the lower levels, losing energy in the process. It is this lost energy that appears as electromagnetic radiation traveling away from the atom.

As the amount of energy lost by an electron when it falls back into a lower-energy orbit in a particular jump varies, so does the color of the radiation it sends out. If, for example, a comparatively large amount of energy is released, it will to our eyes appear as a burst of, say, blue or ultraviolet light. A lower-energy transition may, on the other hand, give rise to a burst of red light or infrared radiation. However, all the colors of visible light – as represented by the colors that make up the spectrum (see pp. 14–15) – together with ultraviolet and infrared light, represent only a small part of the total band of electromagnetic radiation. This band, in fact, extends from high-energy X-rays to low-energy radio waves. The lower the energy of a particular output, the longer its wavelength.

COLOR TEMPERATURE
More important from the photographic viewpoint than the wavelength of different energy outputs, is that the balance of the different colors encompassed by visible light varies between one source of light and another. In photography, the mixture of wavelengths in a particular type of light is often described in terms of its "color temperature." Color temperature is expressed in kelvins (K), which is the internationally agreed scientific unit of temperature measurement. To convert a temperature from kelvins to centigrade, simply subtract 273.

ASSIGNING COLOR VALUES
Imagine an object such as an iron bar being heated from the starting point of ordinary room temperature. When the iron reaches a temperature of 1,000K it sends out radiation of a wide range of wavelengths, but the bulk of it is infrared radiation. Although it cannot be seen with the unaided eye, infrared radiation can be detected as heat.

Continue heating the iron bar and when it reaches a temperature of 3,000K it is still sending out radiation of all types, but now enough of it is in the form of visible light to make the bar glow visibly. Most of the emission from the bar is still infrared radiation, however, and proportionately more red light is sent out than is present in sunlight. As a result, the glow of the bar appears red.

If you were to continue this process, raising the temperature of the iron bar to 6,000K, which is roughly the temperature of the sun's surface, most

The color of daylight can be seen changing throughout the day in the three photographs in this group, which were taken in high alpine country. At sunrise (above) the scene has been dramatically reddened by the atmospheric absorption of blue light, leaving a preponderance of red wavelengths. At about noon time (above right), the snow that is illuminated by direct sunlight appears to be white, but in the shadow areas light reflected from the sky, with a high proportion of scattered short, blue wavelengths, produces a strong blue color cast. In the foggy version of the snow scene (right), the high concentration of particles in the air strongly absorbs blue light and so the overall blue cast is far weaker than in the shadows of the noon-time picture.

of its radiation will then be within the visible spectrum and blue-green predominates. To the eye, the bar appears to be glowing white-hot. Any light source that produces a similar spectrum is described as having a color temperature of 6,000K and in this light colors look perfectly natural. So, color temperature, rather than describing the actual temperature of an object, defines its spectral emission.

If the iron is heated until it vaporizes and the vapor is further heated to 20,000K, its peak emission will be in the ultraviolet. To the unaided eye, the glowing vapor will appear to be a dazzling blue color. Because blue sky light in some conditions has a similar spectrum it is said to have a color temperature of 20,000K. Although color temperature is a convenient way of summarizing the different color mixtures within various types of daylight and artificial light, you must not confuse it with a measurement of heat.

At noon on a clear day, the color of sky light (but not direct sunlight) is affected by scattering by individual molecules (groups of linked atoms) in the atmosphere. A small proportion of sunlight is absorbed and immediately reradiated in all directions by these molecules. Blue light is scattered far more strongly than red, and ultraviolet light even more strongly.

When the air is full of water vapor, dust, or smog particles, it is again the shorter wavelengths of light that are most affected. But because these particles absorb some blue, the light from a hazy sky appears to be less blue than that from a clear sky, and has a color temperature of 8,000K. Light transmitted by cloud has still less blue.

FILM BALANCE

Daylight color film is balanced to a mixture of direct sunlight and light from

a clear blue sky with a few white clouds. But in the morning and evening, when the sun is low in the sky, sunlight has to traverse a great thickness of atmosphere before it reaches your position. The greater absorption of blue light, even when the air is relatively clear, causes the familiar red appearance of the dawn and evening sun and of photographs taken in this light.

Color reversal film must be adapted to the reddish cast of light from a relatively low-temperature artificial source, such as a tungsten-filament lamp. The differing balance of colors in other types of artificial light is sometimes adjusted by means of filters – but illumination from fluorescent lamps, for example, which peaks in certain colors, cannot be given a color temperature.

When you use daylight-balanced film in most forms of artificial light, the result is a predictable reddish color cast, the strength of which varies depending on the spectral composition of the illumination. In the first shot here (left), the subject is illuminated solely by the oil lamp you can see in the frame, which has a very low color temperature. The higher color temperature of tungsten-filament lighting, used in the next image (below left) produces a more natural-looking result, but the coloration is still distinctly warm. In the final picture (below) diffused electronic flash was used as the sole illumination. This light source (accessory flash and studio flash) is balanced to match approximately the color temperature of daylight, and so colors illuminated by it look "natural" in comparison with the other two images.

▽ **Infrared light** reflected from the foliage of a tree shows up as a brilliant magenta in this "false-color" picture. Infrared film not only reveals the presence of infrared radiation in the light reflected from everyday objects but it also gives unpredictable colors from other wavelengths. Hot objects, for example, emit a great deal of infrared radiation, and foliage reflects it strongly. Specialized films respond to the shortest infrared wavelengths – those up to about one micrometer (or micron).

▷ **The color temperature of light sources** ranges upward without limit from below 1,000K (kelvins). At any given temperature a light source emits a wide range of wavelengths, but some are predominant and, therefore, result in an overall color. Hence, the color of radiant light can often be described in terms of color temperature, though this rarely represents actual temperature. Most forms of artificial lighting have color temperatures in the range from 2,000K to 6,000K. Beyond this, daylight becomes bluer as shorter wavelengths predominate. If the blue coloration of some forms of daylight starts to look "unnatural" and too cold, use a warm-up (slightly red) filter on the camera lens. This should not require any exposure allowance.

THE COLOR TEMPERATURE SCALE

1,000K	Candles and oil lamps
2,000K	Tungsten lamps (up to 1,000-watt)
3,000K	Studio lamps, photofloods, "warm-white" fluorescent lamps
4,000K	Clear flashbulbs, blue photofloods, "cool-white" fluorescent lamps
5,000K	Blue flashbulbs, electronic flash, average daylight
6,000K	Bright sunshine with blue sky
7,000K	Lightly overcast sky
8,000K	Hazy sky
9,000K	Moderately overcast sky
10,000K	Heavily overcast sky
11,000K	Sunless blue sky

Forming images

In photography, the formation of an image is dependent on two principal factors – the light reflecting from or transmitted by an object and the camera lens. It is the job of the lens to capture this light – which radiates out from the object in all directions – and, via a complex array of refracting glass elements, each with a different refractive characteristic, to bring its component wavelengths to a common point of focus. Where this light comes into focus inside the camera is known as the focal plane, which, for obvious reasons, coincides with the film plane. When a lens is incapable of performing this task in all situations, faults such as spherical and chromatic aberration may occur.

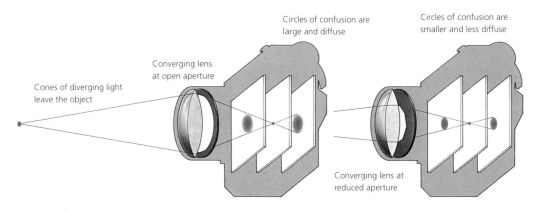

Circles of confusion are large and diffuse

Circles of confusion are smaller and less diffuse

Converging lens at open aperture

Cones of diverging light leave the object

Converging lens at reduced aperture

◁ **Lens aperture** affects image sharpness, as these diagrams illustrate. An object is in focus when rays from each point on it are brought to a point of focus (middle film plane). When the lens is nearer or further from the film, the converging rays from the object form a "circle of confusion" on the film. If the lens aperture is reduced (near left) the cone of rays from the object is narrowed as it leaves the back of the lens. The position of best focus is unchanged, but at other lens-film distance settings the circles of confusion are reduced.

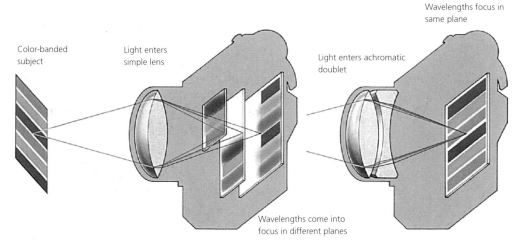

Wavelengths focus in same plane

Color-banded subject

Light enters simple lens

Light enters achromatic doublet

Wavelengths come into focus in different planes

◁ **Chromatic aberration** can cause color fringes around highlights in a photograph. As light enters a lens it is refracted, or bent. In a simple lens (far left) the colored constituents of light are refracted by different amounts and are brought into focus at different points – here, only red is correctly focused in the recorded image (rear film plane). Green would focus nearer the lens and blue nearer still. A combination of lenses, such as the achromatic doublet (near left) made of two materials with different refractive indices, focuses all the colors of the subject at the same point.

In general the photographer can regard light as traveling in straight lines. However, in order to understand its behavior in some circumstances a knowledge of the wave nature of light is helpful. This is basic, for example, in understanding what happens to light when it is polarized.

POLARIZED LIGHT

The color and texture of a surface are revealed when the surface absorbs some wavelengths of the light that falls on it and sends other wavelengths to the eye

or to the camera lens. But this diffuse light can be masked by specular, or mirror-like, reflection. Glossy paper, glass, metal, or still water appear glaring when virtually all of the light falling on the surface is reflected. To cut out this glare, and thus show the qualities of the surface beneath, the photographer has to overcome the polarization of this specularly reflected light.

Although we talk of light as being a mixture of wavelengths, this is merely a shorthand description. Light consists of rapidly varying electric and magnetic

fields. These vibrations are transverse – that is, they move from side to side rather like the waves in a shaken rope. The light from the sun, or from nearly all artificial sources of light, is unpolarized – the vibrations occur at all angles around the line of movement of the ray. Diffusely reflected light is also unpolarized. But after being specularly reflected, light becomes polarized, so that its vibrations are largely in one plane only. A polarizing filter can be aligned to block the light in this specific plane alone, while passing diffusely reflected light.

CONVERGING LENSES

Light waves spread outward from light sources. Because they are spread ever more thinly, the brightness of the light shed by a lamp, for example, falls off with distance – a fact of great significance in studio lighting. For each cone of light rays diverging from the object, a converging lens will form a cone of light rays bending back to form a small disk before diverging again once it has passed that point. The image of an object cast on a screen or film is most sharply focused when the latter is placed where its intersection with each cone of refracted rays forms the smallest possible disk.

The further an object is positioned from a converging lens the closer behind the lens a sharp image is formed. A photographic image is brought into focus (in other words, it forms a series of the smallest possible disks of light) by changing the distance of the lens from the film. The focal length of a particular lens is the lens-image distance when the object is "at infinity" (∞ symbol on the focusing ring) – very far from the lens – and the lens is, therefore, fully retracted.

LENS ABERRATIONS

Nearly all lenses have spherical surfaces. Because of this, and because of the differing wavelengths and refractive characteristics of any package of light rays, simple lenses are subject to a variety of aberrations. In order to eliminate these defects and to reduce as far as possible reflections within the lens barrel itself, which will degrade image quality, a typical modern compound lens for ordinary photographic use will consist of six or more elements – individual simple lenses of differing types of glass (and hence refractive powers) and degrees of curvature.

Spherical aberration is the inability of a lens to focus light from the whole area of the lens. When light rays passing through the center of the lens are recorded sharply, rays passing through the edge come into focus closer to the lens and form a halo around each sharply focused point. Soft-focus lens attachments use a controlled amount of spherical aberration in order to diffuse the image.

Coma is another type of lens aberration. This defect affects off-axis images. Light rays passing through all parts of the lens should be focused to a single point. But when coma is present, a teardrop-shaped patch is formed instead. Coma is hard to cure, especially in a wide-angle lens, and even in a corrected lens it can distort parts of a picture as a result of unsymmetrical light patches being recorded on the image.

LENS APERTURES

Though lenses differ greatly in their construction, focal lengths, and physical dimensions, they are readily compared in terms of the f number, which determines the brightness of the image that the lens will form under particular conditions.

The brightness of the image is essentially the intensity of the light falling onto the film, which is equal to the rate at which light energy falls on a unit area. The larger the aperture of the lens iris, the greater the brightness of the image. On the other hand, the larger the image and, hence, the greater the area over which the light is spread, the fainter the image will be. The size of the image increases with its distance from the lens, which for all but close subjects can be taken to be equal to the focal length of the lens. So the ratio between the focal length and the aperture is a good measure of the brightness of the

△ **Two versions of the same subject** illustrate the type of results you could expect when using a soft-focus filter (above left) and an unfiltered lens (above right). This filter mimics the effects of spherical aberration – a type of defect in which the lens is unable to focus light from all areas of the lens. These shots were taken within a minute of each other and color changes are the result of the filter only.

image that the lens will produce of a scene of standard brightness. When a lens's aperture setting is described as being, say, f4, the diameter of the iris opening is one-quarter of the lens's focal length. The familiar series of f stops (f1, f1.4, f2, f2.8, f4, f5.6, f8, f11, f16, f22, and so on) corresponds to successive halvings of the image brightness, calling for doublings of the exposure time (governed by the shutter) if the same level of overall film exposure is to be maintained. Bear in mind that the larger the f number, the smaller the lens aperture. From this you can see the reciprocal relationship between lens aperture and shutter speed – if you halve the intensity of the light reaching the film and double the length of time that light is allowed to act, exposure remains the same.

The intensity of the light entering the human eye is controlled by an iris that opens and closes in response to the lighting level, in just the same way as light entering the camera is controlled by the lens aperture. The human eye lens, however, focuses by changing its curvature. In photographic terms it is by no means a perfect lens, being subject to nearly all conceivable aberrations. But since only the central part of the visual field is "read" in detail, poor peripheral image quality is tolerable. And the extraordinarily complex "wiring" of the human retina (see pp. 20–1) gives the eye a delicacy and flexibility in color discrimination that no manufactured instrument can hope to match.

Color vision

Our ability to see in color is the result of specialized cells, known as ganglion cells, in the back of the eye and color-sensitive "cones" in the retina. Each cone is sensitive to only one of the primary colors – red, green, or blue. Some ganglion cells are responsible for passing on information to the brain from only one class of cone, while others compare signals from two classes of cone, and either fire (to transmit to the brain) or switch off. Simply, you can think of each cone as either responding or not when light falls on it – much as the microswitches in a computer chip are either open or closed. However, in reality each cone may produce strong or weak signals in response to the differing intensities of color in the light it receives. Many other patterns of cell connections between cones and ganglion cells influence the final information received by the brain.

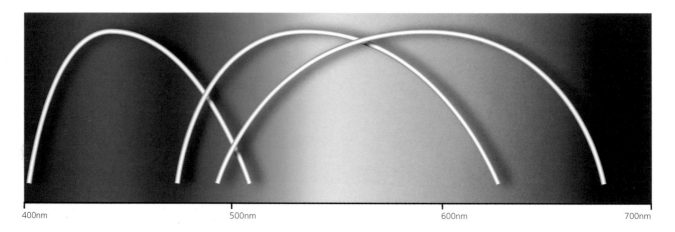

400nm   500nm   600nm   700nm

All human beings are color blind. For, as we have seen on the preceding pages, any given color can be formed by many different mixtures of colored light, among which the eye cannot discriminate. This is because information concerning hue is represented in the eye by the relative strengths of just three different signals emanating from cells sensitive to the red, green, and blue parts of the visible spectrum. As a result of this, three so-called "primary" colors are sufficient to match any hue – a feature that is known as trichromacy.

FORMING AN IMAGE

The cornea, the transparent, horny layer fronting the eye-ball, together with the eye lens, form images of external scenes on the retina, the inner surface of the eye. In some respects, therefore, an analogy can be drawn between the eye and the camera (see opposite), which also has a lens, a "screen" on which the image is formed, and a means of varying focus. Whereas the camera lens is responsible for all the convergence of the incoming light, most of the eye's

focusing power is due to its curved form, and only a little extra power is contributed by the lens. The fact that the eye lens can rapidly change its curvature in order to form sharp images of objects at different distances does, however, give the eye a flexibility in changing focus that cannot be matched by a camera, in which the lens has to be moved back and forth. Without employing special techniques or accessory equipment, it is difficult to produce a film image that shows extremely close and distant objects simultaneously in critically sharp focus.

FROM EYE TO BRAIN

When it comes to the effect of light on the eye's retina, any analogy with the camera ceases. Within the retina are found specialized cells, called rods and cones, which absorb light from the world outside and transform it into electrical signals. These, in turn, cause changes in a long chain of cells leading to the cortex, or outer layer, of the brain. The retina contains several types of nerve cells, which partly analyze the

△ **The responses of three types of cone** enable us to judge the color components of light. There are more than 6 million cones in the eye's retina, each one only $\frac{1}{500}$ of a millimeter thick. The absorption curves of pigments in each type of cone are broad and overlapping. Blue light of short wavelength triggers a strong response – an electrical signal to other cells – from blue-sensitive cones, but little or none from the other two types. Green (medium wavelength) or red (long wavelength) light triggers considerable response from green- and red-sensitive cones, but maximum response to green wavelengths comes from green-sensitive cones and to red wavelengths from red-sensitive cones. The chart above indicates the varying responses of the cones to the colored components of light in nanometers (nm): 1nm=1 thousand millionth of a meter.

information coming from the rods and cones before transmitting it to the brain. Human vision in dim light depends on the specialized cells known as rods, but normal daylight vision and discrimination of color depend on the cones. In the normal eye there are three different types of cone, each containing a different kind of pigment. Each pigment absorbs light of a certain color more strongly than any other. Thus, one absorbs blue light most strongly, another green light, and the third red light. But each type of cone absorbs all colors of light to some extent, and produces an electrical response. As you can see in the diagram opposite, the overlap of response to different colors is particularly marked in the absorption curves for red and green light. The response of, say, a "red-sensitive" cone to a faint red light source could be the same as its response to a bright light from the green wavelength region of the spectrum.

Therefore, if the brain is to sense color there must be mechanisms in place that compare the outputs of the three different classes of cones. In order for the electrical signals to reach the brain, they must pass, via intermediate stages, to specialized ganglion cells. It is the ganglion cells that provide the final output from the retina that is received by the brain.

COLOR AND BRIGHTNESS
In order for the brain to receive sufficient information to be able to discriminate between the myriad hues of light, the cones in the retina must be connected in complex ways to the ganglion cells. For example, a certain type of ganglion cell, known as an "opponent" cell, may receive "excitatory" signals from a cone of one particular type – signals that, had they occurred alone, would stimulate the cell to send a signal to the brain. But

it may "switch off" – in other words, not send a signal to the brain – if the ganglion cell receives simultaneous "inhibitory" signals from cones of another type.

Other types of ganglion cells are known as "non-opponent" cells. With these, excitatory signals from, say, both red-sensitive and green-sensitive cones are received. These ganglions thus signal the brightness of the light, rather than its specific color.

LOW-LIGHT RECEPTORS
Rods occur in the retina along with the cones, but they are only of one type – they are most sensitive to wavelengths in the blue-green parts of the spectrum. That is why in low-light situations, such as in the early dawn or at twilight, when only the rods are functioning, we cannot readily discriminate one color from another. As well, in these low-light situations objects that in daylight would look blue appear much brighter than objects that in daylight would look red.

BLUE SENSITIVITY
The blue-sensitive cones in the eye in fact give little information about the brightness, or intensity, of light, though they are important in our perception of hue. The signals from these cones

appear to be transmitted only to the opponent type of ganglion cells. In an experiment, the red-sensitive and green-sensitive cones can be fatigued by being exposed to nothing but yellow light, because yellow wavelengths excite both of them. Once the red- and green-sensitive cones are fatigued, the subject then becomes wholly dependent on the eye's blue cones, and has difficulty resolving fine detail or detecting flickering in the stimulus light.

For very small details or very faint light, normal vision is like that of a color-blind person who lacks blue cones altogether. This is why it is unwise in color drawings to use thin blue lines, since they will be difficult to distinguish from black ones.

Much of this can be explained by the fact that there are almost no blue-sensitive cones in the center of the *fovea*, which is in other respects the most sensitive region of the eye's retina, and which corresponds to the line of sight. Human beings are particularly insensitive to small or faint blue details when we look directly at them.

LIGHTING INTENSITY
The brightest light that the eye can handle is approximately 10,000 million times as bright as the faintest. The eye

THE CAMERA AND EYE COMPARED

The photographer controls the exposure of the film using the shutter and the iris diaphragm. The eye also regulates light entering it, partly by varying the aperture of the iris. A more important variable, however, is the sensitivity of the cones and rods. Light must penetrate the whole thickness of the retina before reaching these sensitive receptors forming the image-receiving "screen" at the back of the eye. The rods come into play when the light intensity is low. Although highly sensitive, they cannot provide color discrimination, and this task is left to the cones. Information about the intensity and wavelengths of light received by the rods and cones is sorted out in the retina and signals are sent through the optic nerves along pathways leading to higher nerve cells at the back of the brain. A partial cross-over of nerve fibers relays some signals from each eye to both sides of the brain.

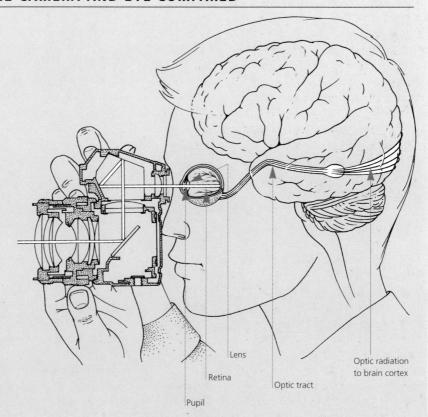

Lens

Retina

Optic tract

Pupil

Optic radiation to brain cortex

must adjust its sensitivity to the prevailing intensity of light falling on the retina, as does an automatic camera. The eye has a variable aperture, known as the pupil, which contracts in bright light and dilates in dim lighting conditions. But the amount of light admitted to the eye can be reduced only by one-sixteenth by the contraction of the pupil. The majority of the variation in the eye's sensitivity to light is due to the automatic adjustment of the sensitivity of the specialist cells and receptors in the retina.

SENSITIVITY CONTROL

Each type of cone in the eye's retina has its own independent sensitivity control. It is this independence that gives the eye the ability to adjust to the color of the surrounding illumination. A piece of paper that looks white when viewed in normal daylight will still look white when we have adjusted to the warm-orange illumination produced by standard, domestic tungsten bulbs – even though the proportion of blue wavelengths in the light is very much lower. But how does the eye make this type of adjustment, which is something that photographic emulsions are incapable of doing?

In normal daylight, which contains all wavelengths in roughly equal proportions, the three types of cones will be about equally sensitive. The piece of white paper will appear white since it reflects a balance of all wavelengths. When we have been under tungsten illumination for some little time, the blue-sensitive cones will become more sensitive than the red-sensitive and the green-sensitive ones. This reaction is in response to the blue-deficient spectrum produced by tungsten illumination. Although objectively the white paper now reflects less blue light than red or green light, the blue-sensitive cones will send the same messages to the brain via the ganglion cells as before.

COLOR ERRORS AND ILLUSIONS

Such adjustments as these have the extremely useful result that we see a given object as being constant in both brightness and hue despite very large changes in the intensity and quality of the illumination under which the object is viewed. However, the adjustments of the eye are not instantaneous and so, occasionally, errors or optical illusions may be created.

One such optical illusion is the complementary after-image. If we stare for a little time at a piece of red paper (such as the red color patch reproduced below) and then look at a white surface (the blank area adjacent to the color patch), we will see a blue-green (cyan) patch that moves around with the direction of our gaze. This effect occurs because the sensitivity of the red-sensitive cones in the eye has decreased through fatigue in the small part of the retina that was stimulated by the image of the color patch. When we now look at the white surface those fatigued cones produce less response than they would normally produce in light containing an even mix of wavelengths – in other words, white light. At the same time, the signals from the blue-sensitive and green-sensitive cones are little changed. Therefore, the overall pattern of signals being transmitted by the ganglion cells to the brain resembles the pattern of signals normally resulting from an actual cyan patch.

Color information from the retina is passed through several intermediate stages before it reaches the occipital cortex, which is the outer layer of the back of the brain (see p. 21). One of the most interesting questions being investigated by scientists working in this field is this: do we have separate neural mechanisms for analyzing color, brightness, saturation, form, movement,

▽ **Complementary after-images** form after a few seconds of viewing any brightly colored scene. Look at the red color patch below under bright light for about one minute or so and then look at the adjacent blank space. You should see a blue-green (cyan) after image. This is caused by the red-sensitive cones becoming fatigued and less responsive while the red-sensitive and green-sensitive cones operate normally. The result is that messages are sent to the brain that correspond to the eye looking at an actual cyan patch.

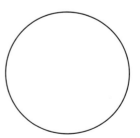

distance, and so on? Experiments on monkeys suggest that there is a region in the brain that is dedicated solely to dealing with an analysis of color. It is possible that there is a corresponding area in the human brain, and that damage to it may account for some of the rare instances of total color blindness (see below).

THE McCOLLOUGH EFFECT

This specific effect indicates that there is a link between an object's form and color at some stage in the brain's processing of signals from the eye. It is very different from an ordinary after-image, for each point on the retina has been stimulated equally by red and green light during adaption to a colored pattern. It suggests that in the human brain there are nerve cells that respond only to a pattern of a particular color *and* of a particular orientation. Such cells have indeed been found in the brains of lower primates.

The apparent color of a tilted pattern – in fact, a bar-shaped pattern – may depend on the relative activity of cells tuned to that orientation, but differing in the color that causes them to respond. While the colored bar pattern is being viewed, cells specific to, say, green bars tilted 45 degrees to the right (and others specific to red bars tilted 45 degrees to the left) grow fatigued. Then a black and white pattern tilted 45 degrees to the right will appear to be pink (the hue complementary to the green of the bars in the original pattern), since the fatigued cells are not contributing their normal response toward our perception of color. Working in the same way, the left-tilted bars in the black and white pattern appear to be tinged with a pale blue-green complementary to the hue of the left-tilted bars in the colored pattern.

Experiments indicate that the colors seem to be "tied" to the bars, since they do not move with the direction of your gaze. Even more remarkably, when the black and white pattern is turned through 90 degrees the bars in a given area will change in their apparent color as their tilt changes. This indicates that it is the alignment of the bars, rather than their position, that is important. This, at least, is one explanation of the curious McCollough effect.

The McCollough effect can be quite long-lasting – if the colored pattern is stared at for about a minute or so in

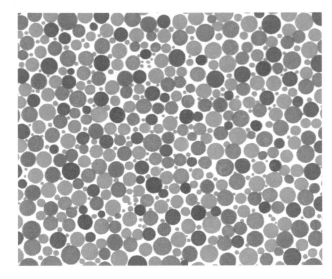

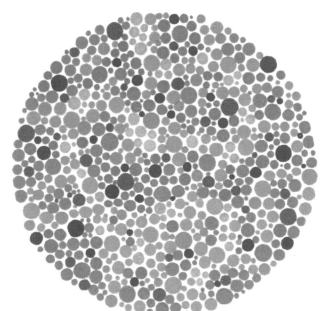

⊲ **Color blindness** is tested with cards bearing pictures like these, made up of multicolored dots. Under proper test conditions, the cards should be held at exactly 3 ft (1m) from the subject, and viewing should be in diffused daylight, not direct sunlight. As well, the illumination should come from behind the subject, not from the sides or the front.

You need to bear in mind that the colors as printed here are not as accurate as those found on the color plates used in the actual tests for color blindness.

The quality of the illumination used for testing is vital, since its intensity will influence subjects' ability to recognize plates, even for those people with completely normal color vision. Marked errors in recognition may indicate color vision deficiency, while slight errors may simply be an indication of carelessness or inattention on the part of a subject.

strong light, the affected cones in the retina can produce this optical illusion for a period of days – that is, if you do not look at the black and white pattern too frequently.

COLOR BLINDNESS

Complete color blindness – a total inability to discriminate between colors, and colors, therefore, cannot be recognized – is very rare indeed. For such people, elements in the external world look to be gray seen against a gray background – not dissimilar to viewing an engraving. However, some deficiency of color vision is not that unusual, especially in men.

About eight percent of all men have some hereditary defect in their color vision, although less than one in two hundred women have the same affliction. Some people (known as "dichromats") appear to lack either the red-sensitive or green-sensitive cones.

The result is that they may confuse, say, red with green or yellow with green and will match any other color given by an appropriate mixture of only two primary colors – instead of three as in people with normal color vision. Another, much rarer, form of color deficiency leads to an inability to discriminate between blue and yellow, and to those with this problem both colors look the same.

Other people ("anomalous trichromates") appear to have three types of cone, but one class of these cones has its peak sensitivity somewhere between the peak sensitivities of normal red-sensitive and green-sensitive cones. Like the rest of us, such people need three wavelengths to match all the colors of the spectrum. The color matches they make are not the usual ones, but there is no sense in which they can be said to be less correct than those made by the majority of people.

Color psychology

The emotional or psychological effects of color are not so easy to measure as the physiological aspects of color perception, yet most of us have color preferences and feel that these affect our moods. Many people find it difficult to live or work in rooms with color schemes that strike them as inappropriate. Colors are thought of as strong or weak, restful or arousing – even heavy or light. Although many such reactions are highly individual, research seems to show that others are widely shared. But our beliefs about color are easily overridden by other sensory experience and the distinctions we make in assigning certain qualities to colors are subtle and elusive.

Laboratory experiments made as long ago as 1907 showed that people agreed about the apparent "weight" of colors. Red seemed heaviest, followed by orange, blue, and green (all similar in weight), then yellow and finally white. Pairs of color patches of identical shapes and sizes looked unstable when the "heaviest" color was on top. Yet this visual impression is not strong enough to influence people's estimation of the weights of different colored objects held in the hand.

SIZE AND TEMPERATURE
Color modifies the apparent size of objects – the colors that look heavy also look small. Among equal-sized squares, red ones look smallest, blue larger, and white largest of all. The French tricolor is normally designed with vertical blue, white, and red bands of equal breadth. But the version used at sea has bands in the proportions 33:30:37 so that, viewed at a distance, the bands will look equal.

The familiar classification of colors into "warm" and "cool"(see pp. 28–9) does not seem to be strongly related to our actual judgment of temperature. In one experiment a blue or green bar at a temperature of 108°F (42°C) seemed warmer to people who held it than a red or orange bar at the same temperature. A test of whether or not the color of lighting of a room affected judgments of its warmth or comfort suggests that illuminating a room with "warm" light is no substitute for heating it.

COLOR AND BEHAVIOR
Industrial psychologists are interested in the effects of color on the performance of the workforce. It has, for example, been claimed that people spend less time in lavatories painted red than in those painted blue. Monkeys have certainly been shown to spend less time in red lighting than in lighting of other colors if they are given a choice. It has been suggested that this is due less to a preference for other colors than to a speeding up of their "biological clocks" in red lighting – the monkeys may simply feel that they have spent longer in the red environment.

If people are asked in experiments to draw a semicircle slowly, they carry out the task better under green lighting than under red, which increases hand tremor

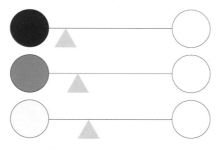

△ **The relative weights** of colors seemed something like this representation to volunteers who were asked to position pointers so that colored luminous disks would appear to balance white ones of the same size. As you can see from the positions of the pivot points, the color red seemed to be the "heaviest" and yellow the "lightest".

△ **Hues in the yin-yang symbols** above show combinations of the type research has established people prefer in color pairs. Contrasting hues, such as green and magenta, are liked, or large differences in lightness if the hues are the same.

– shown also by increased difficulty in holding a needle in a small hole without touching the edges. It seems that red light does have an arousing effect, as is popularly believed, for it increases the electrical conductance of the skin. Yet red light has no appreciable effect on pulse or respiration rates.

COLOR PREFERENCE
Aesthetic reactions to colors, both singly and in combination, have fascinated artists and writers for centuries. Only a few well-controlled scientific studies have been made, but they seem to show a surprising degree of agreement in color preference among different people. When shown specimens of single colors on a neutral gray background, people generally prefer bluish hues, ranging from blue-green to purple-blue. A greenish-yellow is liked least. All colors are liked more when they are lighter.

Research has also established that when people judge the pleasantness of pairs of colors they prefer large differences in hues to small ones, with an even more marked preference for color pairs that show large differences in saturation or brightness.

The impact of abstract color designs can be predicted to some extent from these preferences for single and paired colors. Some psychologists believe that such simple preferences are biologically based and influence even the complex aesthetic judgments we make of paintings or photographs, viewed as color designs.

CROSS-CULTURAL AGREEMENT
Corresponding color terms in different languages may not cover the same range of colors, but the "foci" of the

△ **In the West** and in many other countries around the world, white symbolizes purity and is the preferred color for bridal gowns. However, cultural associations such as this are by no means universal.

▷ **The saffron-colored robes** worn by Buddhist monks may affect the unusually high evaluation of yellow in Buddhist countries such as Thailand, where the priesthood is associated with chastity, a lack of personal possessions, and a shunning of vanity.

terms – the most typical examples of the colors denoted – always agree closely. Many people have reasons in their backgrounds and personal histories that govern their individual associations between colors and other sensory experiences. But leaving aside such personal reactions, some qualities do seem to be generally assigned to specific colors. To an extent, these are influenced by differences of culture or environment (see box below right).

On a "good-bad" evaluation of a range of colors, white is regarded more highly in Asia than in the West. Yellow is evaluated more highly in Thailand than anywhere else – possibly because of religious associations. In terms of potency, green is regarded as a strong color in arid countries. The overall impression, however, is of the uniformity, rather than the diversity, of color "meaning" across cultures. Gray, yellow, and white are usually regarded as weak, while red is almost always seen as being potent and active. Blue is evaluated nearly everywhere as a "good" color. In our perception of color and our responses to it, it would appear that human beings are very much alike.

COLOR AND CULTURAL ASSOCIATIONS

We are more likely to be struck by the variety of responses to color in different cultures than by the similarities. White, traditionally a bridal color in many countries, is the color of mourning in some others. We may have a whole series of cultural association assigned to various colors – for example, white for purity, yellow for cowardice, green for envy, blue for depression, and black for despair. A Westerner is not surprised that in the costuming and make-up of Vietnamese opera, red should symbolize anger, but could hardly guess that white symbolizes treachery and boldness is symbolized by black. Research has shown that, nevertheless, there is much common ground in human reactions around the world. Red, yellow, green, and blue seem to be the "focal" colors for humankind. Before they have even learned to talk, children tend to prefer these colors and to avoid the "boundary" colors lying between them. The names of the focal colors are the first children learn.

Color mixing

The eye contains only three different types of cones, the color receptors found in the retina, and so it cannot respond differently to all the mixtures of wavelengths that make up "white" light that reach it. For example, in relatively pure light, the eye will see a yellow if it receives a narrow range of wavelengths from the yellow part of the spectrum. But it will respond in exactly the same way to certain mixtures of red and green light. White light is a mixture of all the spectral colors; but a mixture of only two wavelengths – one in the red and the other in the blue-green part of the spectrum – can produce a good white.

Not only can a certain perceived color correspond to a wide range of wave-length compositions, a limited selection of colored lights of fixed wavelengths can be mixed in varying proportions to match almost any color. This fact is of prime importance to printers and photographers, since it makes possible virtually all the modern forms of color reproduction on film and paper.

ADDITIVE COLOR FORMATION
If a deep red, deep blue, and a deep green light are projected onto a white screen in the right proportions they will produce white light where they all over-lap (see below right). Varying their relative brightnesses can lead to the production of virtually any desired color. A brown, for example, can be made from a mixture of a dim green light with a slightly brighter red one, with little or no blue.

For this *additive* mixing of colors, a saturated red, blue, and green are described as "primaries". By mixing any two primaries you obtain a "secondary" color. For example, mixing red with progressively more green will produce highly saturated yellow-reds, yellows, yellow-greens, and greens. When a third primary is mixed with such a secondary, the mixture begins to move toward white. These are the unsaturated hues known as "tertiary" colors.

The additive mixing of colors was used in photography by the Scottish physicist James Clerk Maxwell in the 1860s. He recorded the brightnesses of the red, green, and blue lights in a scene on separate black and white negatives, each of which received light of only one color. He made these into positive transparencies and projected each onto a screen with light of the appropriate

color, ensuring that the images were accurately in register. The observer's eyes responded to the mixture of light reflected from the screen roughly as they would have done to the original scene.

PARTITIVE COLOR FORMATION
Because of the inconvenience of making separate images and projecting them in precise register, the type of color system described above is not used today. But *partitive* color reproduction, which depends on part on a form of additive mixing, was the basis of the first commercially successful color photography

and is still used today in color television. When an image made up of multicolored dots is viewed from a distance, the eye cannot resolve the individual spots and their colors seem to be combined. The color perceived in any area of the picture depends on the relative numbers, sizes, and brightnesses of the dots of each color. Therefore, a mixture of red and green dots of equal sizes and in equal numbers would appear as yellow when viewed from a distance. To see how this works in practice, take a magnifying glass and look at any of the color images on this page. Color printing employs arrays

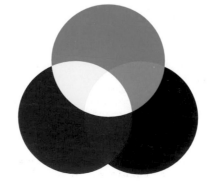

The addition of primary-colored lights gives new colors where they overlap (left). Colors formed by mixing any two of the primaries – red, green, and blue – are called secondaries. The diagram above shows the results of various mixtures of the primaries in light beams projected onto a screen. Below the dark band at the top of the screen, where no light is projected at all, are bands of red, green, and blue where these colors are projected alone. Next, red and green lights are combined to give a yellow band, red and blue lights to give magenta, and blue and green lights to give cyan. Projecting red, green, and blue lights together forms the white band at the bottom of the screen.

COLOR DESCRIPTION

The infinite variety of color can be described with the help of analytical terms based on those first used by artists. Three "dimensions" of color are usually recognized – three characteristics that can vary independently of each other and that can define any possible color.

First, *hue* is the essential quality that distinguishes one color from another – red from blue, for example. Each hue can vary over a continuous range of saturation, or purity – crimson is a highly saturated color, but it can be desaturated by mixing it with white light to make pink.

Second, *saturation* determines the apparent vividness, or chroma, of a color. The spectrum displays perfectly saturated hues, but most of the colors we see every day are highly unsaturated.

Third, a color's *brightness*, its lightness or darkness, depends essentially on the proportion of light reflected by a surface of that color. This, in part, depends on the intensity of the light illuminating it.

Other ways of describing colors also exist. For example, a desaturated color that is lighter than its saturated form is known as a tint, but hue, saturation, and brightness are the terms most essential to an understanding of the reproduction of colors and their interactions with each other – in nature and in photography.

of tiny dots arranged at slightly different alignments so that some of them overlap while others sit side by side. These dots are printed in three colors and black.

SUBTRACTIVE COLOR FORMATION

As explained on pages 14–15, the colors of all objects are due to the subtraction of other colors from the illuminating light. Thus, a patch of red paint sends predominantly red light to the eye because most of the blue and green components in the light falling on it are absorbed, leaving mainly red light to be reflected. When this paint is mixed with

another, each continues to subtract its share of the light and so the mixture reflects still less light. So when red and green paints are mixed, the red paint pigment will absorb a great deal of green and blue light, while the green pigment will subtract yet more blue and and most of the red light. The result will be a dark color.

The colors reflected by the unmixed red and green paint pigments are likely to be far from pure. Instead, they will probably consist of bands of color, which are likely to overlap to some extent. The red will probably reflect considerable

amounts of yellow light and the green pigment is likely to reflect appreciable amounts both of yellow and of blue. Thus, both components reflect some yellow and the color of the mixture is a dark yellow – that is, a brown. This is the basic principle of subtractive color mixing (see below left).

When red paint is mixed with yellow the result will probably be an orange since that is the only wavelength of light that is relatively strongly reflected by both pigments. Yellow and blue pigments, in general, produce a dull green when mixed together – as will yellow and blue filters when they are combined – although, theoretically, these two colors will subtract all the primary colors of light.

Colors are always darkened by subtractive mixing because the resulting mixture necessarily contains less light than any of its components. This was one of the reasons why the Impressionists painted colors in dots and dashes of vivid spectral hues, rather than by using mixed paint pigments.

The overlapping dyes that form the color image on a strip of film must contain the red, blue, and green primaries, but they must not be too dark and dense. Transparent cyan, magenta, and yellow dyes are, therefore, used in photographic films and papers. Cyan absorbs red light and transmits blue and green light; magenta absorbs green light and transmits red and blue; and yellow absorbs blue and transmits red and green. Where cyan and magenta overlap, the mixture formed will be blue; where cyan and yellow overlap they form green; and overlapping yellow and magenta give red. Where all three colors overlap, no light can be transmitted and, thus, black results.

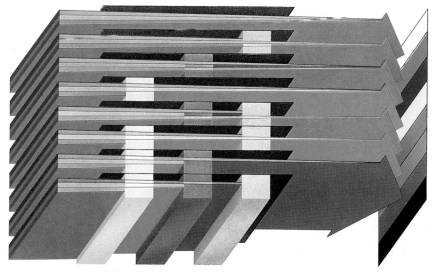

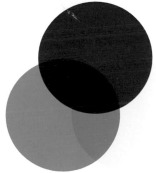

The subtraction of colors from white light by filters or dyes can also form any color. On the left are three filters against a white background. The cyan filter absorbs red light; the yellow blue light; and the magenta green light. Where two overlap, red, blue, or green is passed. You can see this process more clearly in the diagram above, in which a variety of different colors is produced from white light (which can be regarded broadly as a mixture of red, green, and blue) as it passes in turn through various combinations of cyan, yellow, and magenta filters. Magenta and cyan filters pass blue only; cyan and yellow filters pass green only; and yellow and magenta filters pass red only. No light at all can pass through a combination of all the filters.

Color relationships

The key to understanding color is the realization that it is a property not only of objects but also of the light that strikes them. Spectacular evidence of the existence of colors in sunlight is provided by the rainbow, which separates out the colors that, when mixed together, we normally perceive as white light. From the subtraction, addition, and mixing of rainbow hues in thousands of permutations arises our entire world of colors. It is helpful to know how colors relate to each other, and how these relationships can be altered depending on proximity, weather, and lighting conditions, and technical manipulation for deliberate artistic effect.

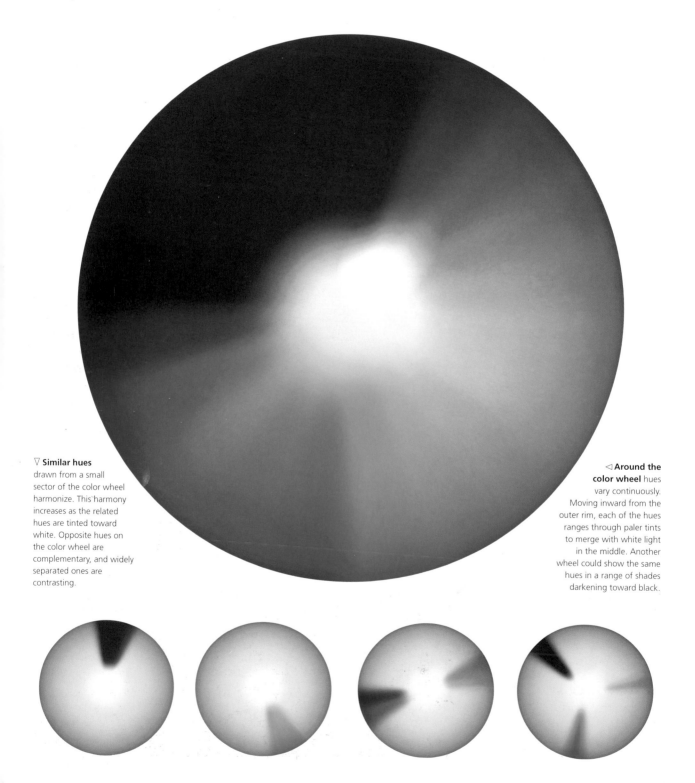

▽ **Similar hues** drawn from a small sector of the color wheel harmonize. This harmony increases as the related hues are tinted toward white. Opposite hues on the color wheel are complementary, and widely separated ones are contrasting.

◁ **Around the color wheel** hues vary continuously. Moving inward from the outer rim, each of the hues ranges through paler tints to merge with white light in the middle. Another wheel could show the same hues in a range of shades darkening toward black.

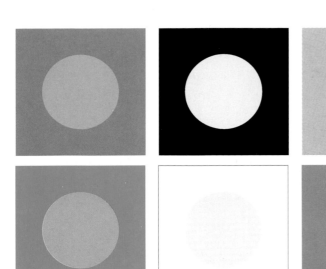

We think of colors as having "natural" brightnesses – yellow as brightest and purple, and perhaps blue, as darkest. It is true that the extent to which any color can be lightened while retaining its purity is limited. So, a rich red paint is of medium darkness, but it can be lightened by diluting it with white to make pink, and it can be darkened by mixing it with black to make reddish-brown.

Yellow can be both very light and bright at the same time. A darkened yellow is a tan, inevitably somber and grayish by contrast with the vividness of a deep blue, even though the blue is low in brightness. Striking effects can be achieved when juxtaposed colors violate our expectations about their relative brightness. We are surprised by an area of olive next to a pink – a green-yellow that is darker than normal adjacent to a red that is lighter than normal.

The perceived lightness of a color depends on its context. A pale color will seem darker in a picture dominated by light colors. Other properties are also influenced by relationships between neighboring colors. Our judgement of hue may be altered when certain colors are juxtaposed. In general, a vivid color will make the color that lies next to it appear more like its complementary color. In this way, red will "induce" a green-blue tinge in neighboring colors.

COLOR CONTRAST AND HARMONY
It is extremely difficult to generalize about the merits of a particular color balance in a picture or color scheme. But there are objective characteristics of

△ **Neighboring colors** can modify not only the effect of a color in a composition but also our judgement of what the color is. Until the surrounding squares are masked off, it is hard to believe that the same color appears in the disks in the upper and lower halves of these diagrams. The disks seem lighter when surrounded by a darker color, and vice versa. Some colors appear to take on a different tinge that is complementary to their neighbors.

color contrast and harmony. Colors harmonize if they are close to each other in hue, saturation, and lightness. Closeness in only one of these aspects may also contribute to color harmony. Pale tints, even of very different hues, can often harmonize successfully, as can very somber shades because they agree in lightness and darkness respectively.

Varying tints of a narrow range of hues – that is, those drawn from a single sector of the color wheel shown opposite

– harmonize with each other. But this is subject to the qualification that small areas of weaker, grayer colors sit uneasily with large areas of more vivid ones, such as small, pale green areas among large, emerald-green ones.

The effect of juxtaposing contrasting colors is to create a vibrancy that is different from the more placid mood created by harmonic colors.

WARM AND COLD COLORS
Reddish hues can be described as warm, bluish ones as cold. Red may owe its suggestion of warmth to its association with the warmth and snugness of domestic scenes lit by candles or fires, while blue is the dominant cast of overcast days and alpine snow scenes.

Reds also seem to "advance" toward the viewer, while blues recede. This may have to do with the greater "potency" that nearly all cultures associate with red (see pages 24–5), but it may also be due to the simple physiological fact that red light is focused less easily than blue light – that is, the eye has to become more strongly curved to bring it to a focus (see pages 20–3). The eye has to do the same to transfer its focus from more distant objects to nearer ones. This may be why red objects seem closer than blue ones that are at the same distance. However, our sense of the "recession" of blue may result from our observation that distant scenes often look blue, an effect created by the scattering of blue light by molecules in the atmosphere.

◁ **When the eye focuses** on the different components of this image made up of superimposed rectangles, the central area seems to retreat and advance. If the eye is concentrated on the outer, darker shade, this appears to predominate. If the inner square is seen as the main point of interest, the outer border appears to recede within the overall pattern of colors.

Working with color

Color and light

Color is constant only under constant light. Outdoors, it changes from minute to minute as the sky lightens and darkens, as the earth warms in the morning or cools toward evening, and as clouds mass or mist gathers. The first essential in handling color is to be aware of this variety in tone and hue.

Many color changes are not even recorded by the untrained eye because the brain has its own built-in filtering system and tends to see colors as it expects them to look. Photographically, however, the inherent color of any object can vary greatly depending on camera angle and on each area's exposure to light. In direct light, one of the simplest ways in which you can influence the colors of your picture is simply to shift your angle of view. By shooting into the sun instead of with it, for example, you can turn white into black. Alternatively, you can wait until the sun itself moves, presenting a reflective surface to the light and the camera instead of one that absorbs most of the available light.

As the different qualities of light play on your subject, shaping and coloring it, you must anticipate the most effective moment to shoot. Even without changing your camera angle, the possibilities can be endless.

△ **Shooting against the light,** so that, in effect, the subject is showing its shadow side toward the camera, and the unusual architecture of this white-painted church darkens into near silhouette. The spire of the church is blocking the sun, preventing direct sunlight from flaring into the lens.

◁ **Shooting with the light** this time and the color of the church is more as you would expect to see it. The sun, in fact, is to the right of the camera position, so the building is being partially sidelit. This helps to throw some shadow onto its façade to produce modeling and depth.

△ **7 am** – The sun has not yet climbed high enough into the sky to clear the trees surrounding this watermill. The shadow is dense, especially on the water, wherever the sun cannot reach.

△ **4 pm** – The sun has now started to move around, more to the rear of the mill, and so their shadows are being cast forward to make an attractive feature on the surface of the pond. Colors are taking on the warmer hues of afternoon.

△ **10 am** – The sun is now higher and has moved around sufficiently to light most of the scene. Although shadows are still present, they are far less dense than they were earlier in the morning and exposure is better balanced overall.

△ **5 pm** – The sun is now approaching the horizon and sunset colors are becoming evident in the sky and edge of the pond. The cloud cover is a little too unbroken for a really spectacular display.

△ **12 noon** – At this time of day the sun is most directly overhead and, although colors can be at their most saturated, contrast is also intense, with surfaces either lit or completely dark.

△ **5.30 pm** – In this dusk shot, the sky is now just below the horizon and the scene is being largely illuminated from daylight coming from an increasingly inky blue sky. Shape is still obvious but the indicators of depth are disappearing.

△ **2 pm** – With the sun lower in the sky than at noon, shadows are now less impenetrable, and form and modeling of the mill and trees have improved. Colors, however, are less impressive.

△ **7.30 pm** – Night has now set in and outside spotlighting is the principal illumination in the scene. Some evidence of halation can be seen due to the length of the manually timed exposure.

Angle of view

Technically, the term angle of view refers to the area of a subject that can be accommodated by a camera lens, which varies depending on its focal length. But in a compositional sense, the view that appears on your film depends largely on the camera position you select and the angle from which you view your subject.

In color photography, the selection of viewpoint is affected by special considerations in additional to general ones such as scale, balance, or perspective. Apart from the angle at which light is striking surfaces, you need to note colors in the background and foreground, which may harmonize or contrast with the subject. Such obvious measures as gaining height to reduce background or shooting upward to eliminate foreground can produce striking changes in shape and patterns, as well as in the colors of objects.

△ **The angle of view** of this photograph has been carefully selected in order to make best use of the surrounding copse of trees. The trees have a remarkably similar shape to that of the roof of the house when viewed from this specific camera position.

◁ **This alternative view** of the same house as that seen above shows the building in a very different light. In order to make the house seem less forbidding, I lay flat on my stomach and shot through a clump of daffodils so that the pale greens and yellows conveyed a more lyrical mood – appropriate for a house where the poet W. B. Yeats once lived.

▷ **A picture seemingly out of nothing** can be made if you keep alert to small details in the environment. From this particular camera angle the room behind the broken window appears as an area of impenetrable black, leaving the viewer wondering what lies beyond.

▷ **A tiny adjustment** of camera position and the whole atmosphere of a shot can change. Now the hole in the window aligns with a window opposite. All the viewer can see from the image, however, is an eerily bright light emanating from a mysteriously broken window pane.

△ **This high-level shot,** looking down on the Piazzetta, Venice, Italy, isolates people promenading in the early evening light and allows them to be studied without conflicting shadows competing for the viewer's attention.

◁ **My object here** was to capture the dynamic lines of this skyscraper in Vancouver. Shot from the base of the building, looking up through a wide-angle lens, the shadowed base of the structure has a solidity that contrasts well with the towering glass walls and their reflections of light-blue sky.

◁ **To gain extra height** for this shot of an Indonesian farmer I climbed onto the roof of my car in order to show him against his paddy-field. In the fading light his face would otherwise have merged into the background vegetation.

△ **A girl's painted toenails** under a trestle table illustrate how an unusual angle of view can not only reveal an interesting symmetry, formed by her legs and the trestles, but also say something in an oblique way about mood and personality.

Light and shade

Except in totally flat lighting, such as that encountered on a heavily overcast day, the camera always records the world as a combination of light and shade, and it is this tonal variation that gives the illusion of three-dimensional form in a two-dimensional photograph or transparency.

Shadows can be used as graphic shapes in contrast to areas of light and color. Shade can also be used to suppress a distracting background and create an intriguing foreground design, as in the example of a glass-and-concrete building below. In other situations, shadows can simply be informative, indicating the direction of light, the time of day, and even the weather conditions. Aesthetically, they can also create powerfully atmospheric effects of drama or mystery.

It is worth remembering that, in color photography, a range of subtle hues not found in bright light can appear in areas of pale shadow. Since shadows are illuminated only by reflected light, your film will often pick up a blue color cast from the sky in these areas, or a cast of another color being reflected from a nearby surface. Conversely, deep shadows surrounding lighted colors can, by contrast, give them a brilliant radiance.

△ **Simple lighting is often the most dramatic,** as you can see in this still life, which has been entirely naturally spotlit by sunshine flooding in through a small window.

◁ **Because unwanted detail** is in shadow, a sense of order has been brought to a picture that otherwise would have looked cluttered. The foreground shadows make an intriguing abstract design, which is entirely in keeping with the geometric architecture of this spacious, modern building. The picture is thus interpretative, rather than merely informative.

△ **Sparkling jewels of reflected sunlight** bouncing back from the white tops of the rippled surface of the water left me with no choice other than to produce this near silhouette. The figures on the jetty, as well as the crossed struts supporting it, were graphically strong enough to make a successful composition relying heavily on light and shade.

▷ **Strongly directional** late afternoon sunlight was used to take this photograph of a suburban house in Sydney, Australia. Note how important the areas of light and shade are in defining the depth and substance of the building and accentuating the detail of its attractively ornate façade and picket fence.

◁ **The mild temperature** of a
Spanish evening is precisely evoked
by the pale shadow of a tree on the
rear wall providing illusory shade
for an old man taking his ease on
a bench.

△ **By taking a highlight exposure
reading** of this scene and waiting
for the cloud to obscure the ball of
the sun itself, color and form seem
to have been flattened to the point
of abstraction.

Monochromatic color

The term monochromatic color seems to embody a contradiction. Pictures are often described as being either colored or monochromatic – incorrectly supposed to mean black and white. Strictly, a monochromatic photograph is one that uses a single color, although the term can be extended to encompass photographs that have a single dominant hue, from any part of the spectrum.

The idea that bright is beautiful is one that is hard to resist. But color need not be vivid to be effective. The literal quality of color – its ability to identify every detail and individual element in a scene – is often criticized by those who believe that black and white photography conveys mood more effectively. But as the photographs here illustrate, monochromatic images show just how powerfully color can itself determine mood and atmosphere.

△ **Daunting weather conditions** have desaturated the vivid red and orange of the steamer and the blue of the yacht's sail to produce a picture full of the atmosphere of the sea. In difficult weather conditions such as these, over- or underexposure will destroy the fragile image and its delicate color content.

◁ **A telephoto lens** was used to isolate just a small slice of an Indonesian paddy-field. Just out of view of the lens, a group of brightly clothed farmers were clearing irrigation channels. If, however, they had been included in the frame, the peace and tranquil atmosphere of the scene would have been shattered.

▷ **Color and detail are so muted** that this lakeside scene has been reduced almost to abstract areas of dense and less dense tone. The background trees were green and the tiny rowboat red, but to capture the atmosphere of a cold, still, mist-shrouded morning I set the camera exposure for the highlights, shooting against the emerging light, to give this overall blue color cast.

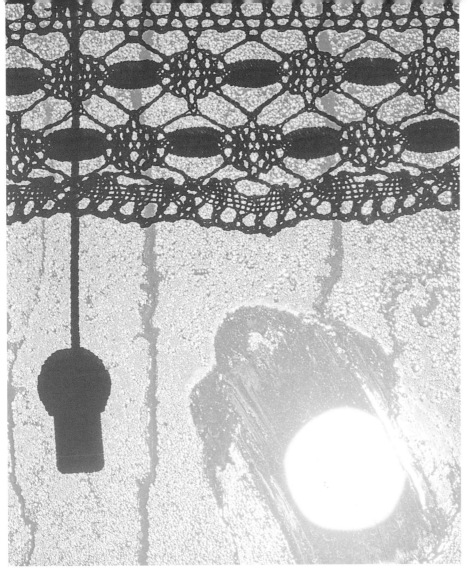

◁ **Photographed through a steamy window** partially cleared by my hand just before shooting, the rising sun has produced an overall yellow color cast on the window and lace curtain. When seen in more normal daylight, the curtain was, in fact, white with a strongly blue pattern.

▽ **The dry Australian outback,** where this photograph of a drover and lamb was taken, is characteristically subtle in coloring, with faded browns, reds, and greens blending into each other. Here, the beige of the stubble mediates between the dark gray of the rider's clothes and the light gray of his horse.

Dominant color

When composing an effective color picture, something more is involved than the considerations of shape, line, tone, texture, or balance that apply to black and white photography. For color itself can set a mood, express an emotion, or appeal to our senses in an entirely abstract way. Colors can be manipulated to create or destroy the illusion of depth and, according to their selection or placement, can establish balance or set up a jarring tension. Many modern painters explore the optical sensations induced by the interplay of colors. In photography, effective color composition is a matter of sensitivity, intuition, and experience, but some basic guidelines can be established.

If you try to cram too many colors into a picture the struggle for dominance may become confusing. The most successful pictures usually has one color that outweighs the rest. Dominance may be established by a large area of subdued color or a smaller area of a bright hue, and it is worth bearing mind that lightness is a relative thing. Lemon yellow, for example, may appear shrill in part of a picture but call no attention to itself in another. Unless the dominant color is itself the center of interest in a picture, it must at least support or enhance it.

△ **Specimen tree** are often placed in gardens and parks where their dominant colors will look best in relation to nearby foliage. The yellow maple in this example as an ideal backdrop to set off both its form and color.

▷ **The subdued coloration of a tree fungus** calls attention to itself only because the framing has excluded potentially competing hues. Texture and form, too, play vital parts in the success of this picture, contrasting the soft, yielding form of the fungus with the hard, fissured texture of the tree bark it has colonized.

▽ **When seen against a neutral background,** the fiery shades of red are able to dominate this composition. The chair, red-banded tights, and eye make-up all help to lead the eye to the model's crowning glory – his red-feathered headdress.

△ **Silhouette lighting** has recorded the subject of this photograph as a two-dimensional shape. The only color there is – the liquid in the glass, which is seen by transmitted light – thus dominates.

◁ **Color creates form** almost unaided in this picture of an upturned boat. With overcast lighting creating little shadow, the rise of the hull is conveyed mainly by the dominant red advancing toward the viewer above the retreating blue color of the sides of the boat.

▽ **With most of the setting** subdued by poor weather conditions in the rapidly gathering dusk, the tiniest touch of bright color, the rear light of the motorcycle, can come to dominate the entire composition.

◁ **The judicious placement of color** in this Indian river scene anchors the eye firmly in the foreground. Only after you have explored the color of the massed blooms in the rear of the boat can you lift your gaze to take in the rest of the early-morning activity.

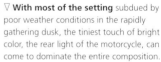

Contrasting color

Contrast in black and white photography is simply the difference between the lightest and darkest parts of a scene. In color, however, while light and shade remain important, the relationships and varying intensities of color become added elements in composition. Boldly contrasting colors, provided they are used in a balanced way, give pictures drama and impact, even without light and shade.

Colors that contrast most strongly lie opposite each other on the color wheel (see pp. 28–9). Although the primaries – red, green, and blue – are themselves clearly demarcated, even sharper contrasts are formed by red against cyan, green against magenta, and blue against yellow. The vibrancy of these combinations has a physiological basis, since the wavelengths representing different colors do not fall into exact focus at the same time on the back of the eye.

Large areas of contrasting colors jostling each other in a picture can often create a restless duality of interest and also tend to flatten out the sense of space in an image, creating pure pattern. On the other hand, a small colorful accent is emphasized by being placed next to a contrasting color and you should attempt to exploit the inherent vitality of such color schemes.

△ **The balloon** is both attractive and easily seen because of its bold design in fully saturated hues. The unblemished sky provides a backdrop of equal density. Maximum contrast between complementary colors is achieved where blue sky meets the sunlit yellow of the translucent airbag.

△ **An energetic vibrancy** has been established by the contrasting colors of electric yellow and various shades of richest green. Color used in this way has given life to the landscape and created an image that demands our attention.

◁ **The quality of the daylight** is so important to the way we perceive colors. Bathed in gentle, bright sunshine, the petal of this flower glow at us out of the frame, and they are thrown even more to the fore by the contrasting out-of-focus green of the background.

◁ **Color affects mood.** Our immediate reaction on seeing this old fishing boat is a smile. The bold use of blocks of contrasting color – brought about by the chance availability of paint colors at any particular time – speaks of a sunny Mediterranean setting. It's even possible to see the progression of work on the boat – the wheel house receiving more recent attention than the hull.

▷ **Color saturation** can high-light color contrasts that might otherwise be unremarkable. Here, the more saturated terracotta hues of the shed standing out boldly against the less-saturated blue of the sky.

Color harmony and discord

Mood can be established as easily by color harmony as by color contrast, but it is often a gentler mood. Harmonic colors are grouped closely together on the color wheel (see pp. 28–9) and make up only a restricted palette, consisting usually of two colors in desaturated form. The absence of strident or aggressive colors, however, makes it easier to appreciate fine distinctions between similar hues.

Although harmony is partly a matter of inherent color characteristics, it can also be achieved by tone, scale, or placement. If a calm, restful atmosphere is required, it is often possible to subdue contrasting colors either by dissipating them in strongly reflective light or by slightly underexposing the scene to produce a low-key picture.

Color discord can be created by placing contrasting colors together that are uncomfortable to look at. But dissonance can sometimes be useful as harmony, and although some colors are thought to be inherently discordant, they can be used effectively in the right mixtures and proportions.

△ **The dark, underexposed** bulk of the shoreline in this dusk shot anchors the harmonious shades of pink and purple so distant it has turned almost to lilac.

△ **Haze has blended** the widely differing shades of green of this high-country farmland into a harmonious composition. If bright sunshine had been a factor in the picture, the sharply demarcated shades would have reduced the impact of the blue haze that indicates depth and distance.

◁ **Color harmony exists** everywhere in nature, and even the colors introduced by man seem, in the process of time, to blend into their surroundings. Once a bright turquoise color, this faded and rusted water pipe lives amicably with the greenish-brown seaweed in a harmony increased by mutual reflections.

△ **Harmony can be the result of cultural association,** as in this photograph of a rowing boat hauled up on a beach, its hull painted yellow and blue, the colors of sunshine, sky, and water.

▷ **This busy market scene** in South America is, to Western eyes, full of color discord – reds against blues, against greens, against yellows, and so on. The effect of all this color is to signal strongly the "other-placeness" of the scene.

▽ **This garish display** of fully saturated and competing primary colors has had a type of harmony imposed on it by the repeating shapes of the displayed shoes. Rather than repelling, the effect is to encapsulate the simple pleasures of a seaside vacation.

Picture composition

Composition and line

Composition is often regarded as something daunting by those new to photography, but it is nothing more than the organizing of all the elements you see in the viewfinder so that the final picture conveys your intention. Though it usually implies order, it could equally imply disorder. Angle of view is fundamental to composition, since it determines the relative emphasis given to objects as well as the selection of the picture area itself. Equally important in composition is your use of such subject attributes as line, proportion, tone, and texture.

Line is important both in its strict meaning as a linear mark or outline and in its general sense of the direction taken by the viewer's eye when looking at a photograph. A good composition often leads the eye to a single main subject and then lets it explore the rest of the image. In pictures with depth, movement may be from the foreground, through the middle ground, and then to the background. With pictures full of surface interest, movement of the eye may be more circular.

◁ **A simple circular frame** acts as a tunnel, directing the eye to the anxious concentration on the boy's face as he struggles to maintain his grip on the climbing frame. The surface characteristic of the composition is emphasized by the out-of-focus background.

◁ **Line, scale, color, and tone** all combine to mark the seated figure out as the main point of interest in this shot. Although subdued by mist, the scene is full of depth and detail, and the sweeping curve of road-marking "cat's-eyes" leads your attention to the approaching figure in the middle ground and then through to the distant warehouses.

◁ **Rocks lead from the bottom** of the frame, like two stepping stones carrying your attention toward the face of the subject. By crouching down and using a wide-angle lens I have exaggerated the effects of perspective and helped to emphasize the balancing effect of the color and texture of the cotton top.

△ **The curved line** of the rail draws the eye deep into the composition, initially past the statues and nude model, leaving you in no doubt that the diminutive figure of the artist is the principal subject.

▽ **A length of coiled hose** and a shallow depth of field give an effective surface composition in which the center of interest is the expressions on the faces of the two young boys. The out-of-focus background tends to thrust the figures forward in the frame.

Balance, position, and scale

Rules of composition in photography are useful guidelines, even though, like all rules, they are made to be broken. A fundamental principle is that colors, lines, and shapes should be balanced so that they help to convey the main statement of the picture instead of causing conflict. Balance need not necessarily mean symmetry, however. Two equally dominant colors will compete for attention, but if colors, shapes or areas of differing sizes or strengths are positioned in the right way they can provide a more effective pictorial balance.

The position of the horizon is a significant factor in landscape shots. If the horizon is in the middle of the frame the effect tends to be static. Altering the proportions within the image – by moving the camera down to emphasize the ground or up to emphasize the sky – will give a more dynamic composition.

On a less obvious level, the classical divisions of space used in paintings can be equally effective in photography. If you mentally divide whatever you intend to photograph into thirds, both horizontally and vertically, objects positioned on these divisions, and especially at intersections, are given added emphasis. This can be particularly useful in positioning people for portraits.

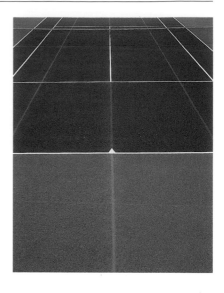

▷ **The off-center passenger ferry** in this picture helps by adding a sense of vitality to the composition, which, with the horizon almost in the middle of the frame, could have looked overly static had the subject been place more conventionally.

△ **A small pyramid of white** at the intersection of lines on a tennis court becomes a focal point in a pattern that balances somber browns and greens. Scale, perspective, and color are all in perfect counterpoise and the recession of perspective lines is so strong that at first you don't even notice the net bisecting them. The illusion of the white lines of the serving court floating above the fainter brown lines adds further optical interest.

▽ **An unusual camera angle,** looking directly upward with a wide-angle lens, creates an enclosed atmosphere as the all-round view is cut off by towering glass-fronted buildings and produces a satisfying sense of balance.

△ **A low horizon** emphasizes the sunset colors of the sky in this twilight beach scene. Had the donkey and rider been positioned much to the right or left, they would have become lost in the heavy foreground shadow, thus making their central position ideal in this example.

◁ **Even on a small scale,** the right combination of colors in the right position can hold the eye, as this no-entry sign on a goods yard door demonstrates. Placed at eye level, the contrasting colors of red, white, and blue against a light brown background produce maximum impact and symmetry.

▷ **The careful placement** of the only vertical features in this desert scene is vital for defining the various planes in the image. The slight rise in the terrain that is hiding the base of the palms effectively becomes the horizon.

Point of interest

It is not always necessary for photographs to have a single or dominant point of interest to be successful; there are times when it is the overall effect of a scene that counts. What is true, however, is that whether or not a single area of the frame is emphasized, the most effective pictures are those that make a single statement. If, for example, an artist decides to use several points of interest, they are usually of varying importance and are carefully related so that they do not compete for attention to the detriment of the whole.

As a general rule, the point of interest of a photograph should be placed somewhere off-center in order to produce a sense of movement and tension. A color accent can often provide the point of interest, but a whole range of other devices can be used to focus attention on the main message of the composition – angle of view, for example, or a change of scale, perspective, light, movement, texture, or pattern. People, particularly when they are caught in the act of moving, can exert an attraction that is out of all proportion to their scale in a picture through the viewer's tendency to relate to them. In this case, human interest then becomes the main focus of attention.

△ **Color and placement** draw immediate attention to this sun umbrella and chairs. The sand is such a neutral tone that the eye craves the color impact of the boldly positioned beach furniture.

△ **An overcast day** sealed in the available light and saturated the colors to give added brilliance to a golden fountain that seems to glow in the center of a formal pool. The fountain, the immediate point of interest, also directs attention to the the palace in the middle ground and then to the somber, mist-shrouded hills behind. The three-dimensional effect created by the foreground prevents the palace looking like a flat façade.

▷ **A low camera angle,** halfway up the valley wall and looking up at the simple country church, has made sure that the building becomes the main point of interest in this picture. Perched on the horizon like this, the background is an uncomplicated skyscape, but notice that the spire of the church has been carefully lined up with the dip in the cloud sitting just above it.

◁ **The framing of this shot** leaves the viewer in no doubt as to the principal point of interest. Having set the camera up on a tripod and adjusted the focal length of the zoom lens to include symmetrical sections of balustrade to frame the overall scene, all I had then to do was wait for the boat to reach precisely the right spot before pressing the shutter release.

▽ **Frozen by the use** of a fast shutter speed, the viewer's attention is immediately riveted on the graceful form of a dancer stopped cold in mid movement. Emphasizing the dancer as the focus of attention in the composition is the single beam of window-shaped light falling at the figure's feet.

◁ **A chance play of light** has illuminated vividly the painting of a hen and its chicks, so that the artist and his family seem almost transfixed by the image. The picture has become an imperative feature in an otherwise over-complicated domestic scene. In a sense, it does not seem to belong to the room at all, its white contrasting strongly with the dark background.

Shape and silhouette

The camera and modern film emulsions are the most accurate pictorial recording device we have at our disposal. Almost no complexity of composition, line, color, tone, or texture is beyond its descriptive capacity. But it can also be used to simplify the world around us, reducing detail and accentuating the most basic element of objects – their shape. The use of shapes as easily recognizable pictorial codes ranges from road signs to advertising; people we are familiar with can be recognized by their shape alone when they are still too far away for color or detail to be distinguished.

The ability for the camera to manipulate shape is crucially important in color photography, where sharply defined areas of strong color often have the effect of flattening form and emphasizing outline. But the boldest, most graphic, shapes of all are created by silhouettes, in which all surface detail is suppressed in favor of shape. When they are photographed against the light, and with no exposure compensation taken into account, objects as well as people can look as two-dimensional as cardboard cut-out images, making us instantly and powerfully aware of their essential message.

△ **By carefully aligning** the subject's head with the still intense setting sun you can create this attractive rimlighting effect. Unless you judge exposure carefully, however, the light flaring around the subject is likely to pick up some surface detail around the edges.

△ **When using window light** to take a silhouetted photograph, take your light reading from the outside scene. Depending on the type of camera you are using, you may then have to lock this reading into the camera before recomposing the shot. Open up a stop or two if you want to record some subject detail.

◁ **The effects of a sea mist and pollution** have obscured all surface detail on the superstructure of this bridge and the towering buildings beyond, leaving nothing but the evocative power of shape to define their presence.

▷ **Flat areas of subtle pink** on a background of pale blue make this picture close to a purely abstract design in the shape of flamingoes. Because the photograph has been taken against the light, there is no modeling on the bodies and so their form is described entirely by our knowledge that birds are rounded and by the shape their feathers take.

△ **A wind-sculpted line of trees** on the brow of a hill makes a series of fascinating shapes when seen like this – about three full stops too dark against a well-exposed scene of a distant bay.

▽ **A simple picture conveys through shape alone** all that is necessary for us to know about this stooped old man searching on the beach for shellfish at low tide. The dog, and the diamond shapes reflected within its legs, balance the composition, and the limited color palette provides atmospheric support.

Form and modeling

Creating a lifelike and convincing illusion of three-dimensional form on the flat surface of a frame of film by means of the camera's fixed, single eye is one of the most exciting aspects of photography. Since bright, "warm" hues seem to advance toward the viewer, while dark, "cool" ones seem to recede, color can itself sometimes indicate form. But in suggesting the weight and volume of an object, what that object would actually feel like if you could touch it or pick it up, lighting is the crucial factor. This is because our visual memory of form is prompted mainly by the way in which varying surfaces are differently illuminated by light and by resulting tonal gradations.

Sharp, clearly defined contrasts of light and shade produced by strong side-lighting can convey the powerful angles of geometric objects. But more subtle forms tend to be flattened by overlighting or lost in deep, featureless shadow. The rounded contours of living things are best conveyed by the gentle modeling of diffused lighting. In the studio, you can achieve diffused lighting by introducing translucent material between the light and subject; outdoors, you may need to wait for a veil of cloud to cover the sun before shooting.

△ **Photographs of the male form** often benefit from a lighting scheme different from that used for the female form. Here, the well-defined musculature of the subject has been accentuated by using reflected, as opposed to diffused, lighting from a silver-colored flash umbrella.

△ **Muted colors** and the use of weak, diffused directional lighting reveal the subtleties of this classic Greek sculpture, giving it substance and solidity while softening the cold smoothness of the marble. This is often the perfect light for the female form, and for delicate sculptures. The shadow on the wall behind helps to give the picture depth.

▷ **Even utilitarian, domestic fixtures** can take on a type of sculptural quality if they are photographed in a sympathetic and an appropriate light. This old-fashioned fixture has been lit predominantly by window light reflected from a building opposite. It is interesting to note that where light merges into shadow the form of the subject is most clearly evident.

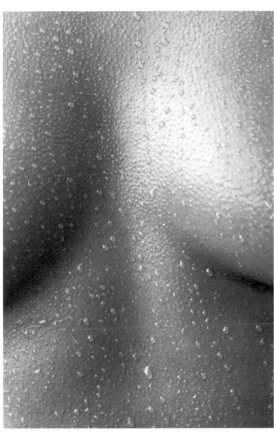

◁ **A subtle range of tonal gradations** define the breasts and partial torso depicted here. Moisture on the skin reflects a soft sheen in places, contrasting with the dark shadows under the model's breasts, while the water droplets act as tiny lenses, returning isolated highlights.

△ **The smooth red shapes** of tomatoes in a box are given three-dimensional form by the color and texture of the background and the contrast between shadows and toplit surfaces. As a result, the tomatoes have a crisp roundness that appears tangible.

▽ **A moderately slow shutter speed** (⅒ second) has caused the frothy tops of these small waves to blur and mold themselves into more substantial-looking organic forms. The shutter speed needed to create this type of effect depends on the speed the subject is moving.

Tone and hue

In photography the effect of a composition depends largely on the interest of its tonal variations. Tone in this context simply means the range of lightness and darkness within a picture. This range can extend from black to brilliant white depending on the reflection or absorption of light. Tonal gradations are vital in suggesting three-dimensional form; dramatic tonal contrasts emphasize the solidity of forms; more gentle contrasts reveal their subtleties in diffused light. Color photography extends the tonal range because variations of brightness can be produced by changes of hue as well as of light intensity. Inherently, colors have differing brightness values. Of the four most distinctive colors – red, blue, green, and yellow – blue is the darkest and yellow the lightest. But within each of these colors are countless individual hues with subtly different intensities.

Tone becomes a far more important compositional element than hue in monochromatic pictures and in dim or misty light, which tends to blend colors and disguises their differences. However, sensitivity to both tone and hue is needed in order to produce effective photographs.

◁ **Differing yellow hues,** ranging from the orange of the deckchair through to the umber-colored sand and the lemon of the furled umbrella, are the main compositional elements in this deceptively simple photograph.

◁ **The range of hues** in this image of the Great Barrier Reef is the result of the varying depth of water and the nearness of the coral to the surface. The scene is given additional interest by the variety of harmonic colors, ranging from the dark blue of the channel between the reefs to the hues of the shallower water where a turquoise color has started to emerge.

◁ **Rows of 19th-century** houses in a British industrial town, wrapped in the smog and sea mist of a bright winter morning have been reduced to a tonal pattern ranging from near-black to near-white highlights. Clear light would have shown up many more colors, especially the slate-gray of the roofs, but the scattered light has produced an overall blue color cast instead.

▽ **Early morning light** on an estuary at low tide has reduced the colors of the sand, sea, and distant grass to simple tones of blue-gray and beige. The tones in the water and on the sand change in value according to the way the light is either absorbed or reflected. Including the lone figure in the shot gives the landscape an immediate sense of scale.

Texture

In the same way that form describes the volume and three-dimensional quality of your subject, so texture describes its surface characteristics, adding a further facet to a picture by telling us what the subject might feel like if you could run your hand over it.

While largely holding true for black and white work, the truism that raking, oblique lighting best reveals texture needs to be treated with a degree of care in color photography. Rather than adhering slavishly to rules regarding styles of lighting, it is best to bear in mind that the quality of the illumination should always match the subject. Shadows cast by harsh sidelighting may, for example, suit the character of a piece of heavily corroded metal or of an old man's weatherbeaten face, but not necessarily the creamy skin of a child. Texture is an important way of indicating depth, but hard shadows may destroy subtle hues.

When texture in crucial to the success of a photograph, the best type of lighting to avoid is that from a heavily overcast sky, since this produces little in the way of light and shade. Likewise, head-on lighting has a flattening effect on texture, as does heavily diffused studio lighting.

◁ **Texture and color** play major roles in describing the form of this tree trunk. The inverted V formed by the shadow area is the only discernible shape, and the soft directional light brings out a play of yellow and green against purple-tinged shadow areas that would have been lost in stronger light. Such shapes suggest other forms – the scaly limbs of a giant.

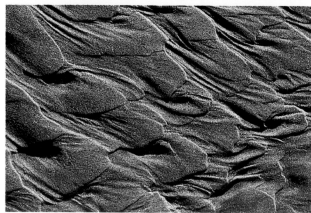

◁ **A bale of wool** has been transformed from a mundane object into a dramatic one by an intriguing combination of textural surfaces. Indirect sunlight striking the shining golden fiber of the bale has accurately revealed fines variations in texture, conveying the tactile sensations of taut wire, harsh fiber, prickly hair, and soft wool behind a film of smooth plastic.

◁ **Texture is on two levels** in this picture of corroded metal. First, there is the minutely pitted base metal, its texture defined as tiny alternating areas of brightness and shadow. Then there is the surface texture of bubbling, peeling paint, whose surface texture is made tangible by the low angle of the light coming from above.

▷ **Revealing texture** can be a function of viewpoint and focal length as anything else. In this example of a sentinel-like pine trunk, a shot framed from further back would not have revealed the overall stippled texture of the bark, and the composition would have been more remarkable for its monochromatic use of color.

◁ **Irregularities of color** in the mineral composition of the sand give some textural information in this photograph. Viewed more broadly, however, and it is the areas of shadow filling the tiny valleys, dips, and craters carved by the retreating tide that really tell us what this stretch of wet sand looks like.

Pattern

Patterns surround us all, reflecting not only our own instinct for order but also the repetitive sequences to be found in the natural world – dappled, or mottled, striped, spotted, or grained. When viewed objectively, it is surprising how often human activity, both in the countryside and in the more intensely developed environment of towns and cities, results in the creation of unintentional pattern.

Photographs that use pattern as their sole subject do not pretend to be anything more than decorative, but they can be intriguing nevertheless. This is especially true when the pattern is created by an accident of viewpoint or lens focal length, for example, or a momentary trick of light and shade. Apart from delighting us by their sheer novelty value, such pictures sometimes exert a curious power – perhaps because they show a design underlying the apparently random surface of things.

Pictures of patterns taken in black and white tend to be abstract in content. Their main interest lies in the vitality and texture given to the picture surface by repeating tonal accents. Color patterns, however, tend to arouse a more emotional response in the viewer.

△ **Camera angle is important** to accentuate the patterns in this wall comprised of logs. The pattern of the grain is one repeating element, as are the upright logs themselves, but a high viewpoint is needed to see the pattern of the top cut surfaces.

▷ **Humans create patterns** wherever they work or settle. Sometimes planned as decorative motifs, they are more often, as here, the result of chance or convenience, following and emphasizing the contours of the land. The patterns produced by these transformations may show up best in diffused light, though shadows give added interest provided they do not conflict.

▽ **Neatly arranged bottles** have been stacked to form an entirely symmetrical pattern, one that has been enlivened by a network of shadowy black lines and a composition that has an overall sloping effect.

▷ **The interplay of light and shade** on the skeletal shapes of winter trees leads the eye in and out of the composition. The trees, rather than creating a wall, are more like a veil subduing the intrusion of background detail.

△ **Repeating geometric patterns** are a feature of much modern architecture. Reflections in the glass-sided monolith fall neatly within the squares of glass, accentuating the inherent pattern of the structure.

◁ **The nature of the underlying terrain** dictated the pattern that can be discerned in these Indonesian paddy-fields. In order to retain the water necessary for the young rice shoots to grow on the steeply sloping hillsides, paddy walls have to be built, as they can be seen here, in regular and repeating patterns.

Perspective

Perspective in the two-dimensional art of photography recreates the real world's third dimension – its depth. As has already been demonstrated (see pp. 56-7), the tonal modeling provided by light and shade can suggest depth and volume in an individual object or person. The illusion that one subject element in a photograph is farther back than another, however, is created by four main types of perspective.

Of particular interest in color photography is *aerial perspective*, which is the tendency for colors or tones to become lighter and bluer as they recede due to atmospheric diffusion. *Overlapping forms*, one partly obscuring another, are a second indicator of depth. In *diminishing scale*, objects look smaller the further away they are. Finally, *linear perspective* is the gradual converging of planes or lines as they recede from the camera.

In the same way that a strong pattern will tend to flatten the appearance of a picture, so all these types of perspective can be used to give pictures a sense of depth. A subsidiary indicator of depth is known as *selective focus*, which is the knowledge we have from our own experience that a sharp and an unfocused object must be on two different planes. This type of focus differential is largely a matter of choosing an aperture that produces a limited depth of field.

△ **The principal indicator of depth** in this scene is the curving line of fence uprights, which act as signposts to lead you through the landscape to the farm buildings in the middle ground and then on to the more distant mountains. The tonal contrast between the buildings and the mountains also enhances the three-dimensional effect of the composition.

△ **Linear perspective** is very evident in this photograph of a grand, large-scale interior. The lines of long tables, which we know should be parallel, appear to converge strongly as they recede from the camera. Echoing and reinforcing this visual phenomenon, the pattern of the floor tiles also appears to converge.

▷ **A sense of depth has been conveyed** in this photograph of an English fishing village by selecting a camera angle that ensures all of the image planes – the foreground, middle ground, and background – are full of subject elements. Through this device, the eye is taken back from the foreground tangle of ropes, over the sea wall to the railings separating the roadway from the distant cottages and background foliage.

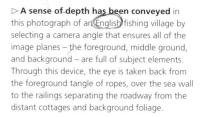

▷ **In this complicated** collection of buildings, rooflines, walls, and courtyards, it is the numerous overlapping forms that prevent the scene from appearing two-dimensional. Another indicator of depth is to be found in the relative sizes of the windows in the near and far buildings.

◁ **This compelling picture** forces the eye to pass between the uprights and across the footbridge. The apparently converging cables supporting the bridge are one indicator of depth, as is the diminishing scale. This is provided not only by the dwindling cross-members, but also by the uprights on the far side, which appear tiny.

△ **Aerial perspective** in this picture of Bavarian mountains carries the eye of the viewer back from the brighter colors of the foreground vegetation to the overlapping background peaks, their color dissipated by atmospheric haze and distance. Haze caused by the presence of ultraviolet light is common in mountainous regions.

Backgrounds

While framing can be used to hide a distracting foreground, it is often more difficult in outdoor photography to eliminate an unsatisfactory background. Selective focusing with a wide aperture or long lens can help to isolate your subject from its setting, and a slow shutter speed will provide a similar effect through blur if there is movement in the background. Lighting is another means of control, but bear in mind that a background need not be subordinate, as the name implies. Finding a suitable existing background is sometimes only a matter looking and assessing its importance to your composition.

Because its purpose is to support a subject, not overpower it, a planned, as opposed to a found, background involves an important creative decision. The background can be dramatic, softly atmospheric, or narrative, placing the subject in context. Its lighting should generally be one stop lighter than on the subject. Paper rolls provide convenient plain backdrops, and elaborate subjects often look good against them. Black or white, although sometimes effective, should be used with caution, since it can make subjects appear to sink into gloom or float on the surface. Things normally do best against a solid base that has tonal variety.

▷ **A portrait background** can range from a damp, peeling wall to an elaborate painting, as in this shot of a member of the London Company of Fishmongers, which was taken with a single electronic flash at f8 using a 150mm telephoto (on a medium format camera). The background is definitely narrative here, with the painting's subject matter giving the uniformed figure a proper context.

◁ **Selective focus** becomes an advantage when photographing animals, which often have to be picked out from backgrounds that provide them with natural camouflage. This shot, taken with a long 400mm lens (on a 35mm camera), has isolated the impala while taking in the delicate blades of grass that perfectly match the animal's alert nervousness.

▽ **The main subject** can often be effectively presented as the background, as in this shot of the New York skyline, its shapes echoed by the silhouettes of battered timbers on a Brooklyn wharf. Sympathetic shapes linked in this way will enliven the most prosaic of views.

▷ **Window light** was the only illumination for this portrait of a sculptor posed in front of the cluttered shelves of his studio. Choosing the right background can greatly assist your subjects to relax and to express something of their personality – if the subject here had been transported to the anonymous environment of the photographer's studio much information would have been lost to the viewer.

▽ **A plain background** in a studio set-up does not have to be uninteresting. For this still-life composition, I decided that I wanted a subdued backdrop for the collection of china, but did not want to use a length of featureless background paper. Instead, I opted for an old tarpaulin to add textural interest as well as tonal contrast, without running any risk that it would overpower the subject.

Capturing movement

The camera may seem better equipped to arrest movement than to convey it. If your judgement is bad, the result will be the paralysis of a subject that was full of vitality. Yet if properly understood, the techniques for capturing movement can produce images bursting with life. The basics are simple. You can show movement via a sequence of pictures that add up to a visual story. Alternatively, you can show movement by selecting an exposure that will record, as a blur, movement either by the subject or by the camera itself. And, finally, you can take a sharp picture at such a vital moment that the imagination of the viewer completes the drama. Sometimes movement can be conveyed by pattern alone or by the force of perspective. Color adds its own impact to photographs of moving subjects, and colors can be radically altered by the movement of highlights into shadows during long exposures. If you want to record only slight blur, calculate the shutter speed that would freeze the action and then shoot at half that speed.

△ **Selecting a shutter speed** of ⅛ second and panning the camera during the exposure have turned the horse and rider into a ghostly apparition. Note that the blurring and streaking of the highlights have started to "eat into" the darker toned areas.

▷ **If you can match** your speed to that of the subject, you can use a slow shutter speed to freeze fast-moving action. Shot from a helicopter traveling at about the same speed as the boat, a shutter speed of ¹/₂₅ second would have been sufficient to freeze its movement. However, to prevent vibrations from the airframe affecting image quality, I opted for a speed of ¹/₅₀₀ second instead.

◁ **Neon lights** can be easily transformed into an attractive, fantasy pattern of lights at night just by waving the camera about while keeping it approximately directed at the main light source. A shutter speed of 2 seconds was used here.

△ **Precise timing** is needed to record an image such as this, which manages to convey both motion and formal rigidity.

▽ **When panning the camera** you have to select a shutter speed that will maintain the appropriate level of subject detail while reducing all stationary parts of the scene to an attractive blur. In the example here, ¹/₆₀ second produced the right balance.

◁ **An illusion of movement** was created here when an 85–210mm lens was foused on the shirt of a stationary motorcyclist. Then, during the ⅒ second exposure, the lens was steadily zoomed from its longest to its widest setting. This technique needs some practice to perfect.

▷ **When clearly defined** subject detail is important for the type of picture you want to record, select a shutter speed that stops all movement dead in its tracks – for this picture, ¹⁄₂₅₀ second. However, don't forget about depth of field – if your preferred shutter speeds means using too wide an aperture, a different form of subject blur may be introduced.

▽ **A combination** of camera and subject movement during exposure produced this interpretative study of motor bike riders at sunset. The bike was not traveling fast, but a shutter speed of ⅒ second and a slow pan give all the excitement of motion while sacrificing little in terms of subject detail.

◁ **Panning,** to keep up with the plane, and a rapid zoom (with an 85–210mm lens), to distort the shape of the sun flare, are the two techniques employed in this intriguing image.

▽ **A radical approach** to exposure is required for an image such as this. The subject was running past the camera position but to produce this degree of blurring I selected a shutter speed of ½ second. To compensate for such a slow speed, an aperture of f16 was needed. And to ensure that the brick forecourt and wall were pin-sharp, the camera was set up on a firm tripod.

Color in close-ups

Photography at close range can sometimes produce unexpected color pictures, particularly where magnification reveals an unsuspected richness of color in things so small they would normally pass unnoticed. As some of the examples here show, deep color saturation is often evident in a masked-down area of a subject because it does not have to compete with nearby highlights or light sources.

Although close-ups taken with ordinary lenses are perfectly possible, the capacity to reveal color and detail is extended in macrophotography, which allows subjects to be recorded at life-size or above. An array of equipment, including bellows, extension tubes, and macro lenses, is available to achieve this. However, many modern zoom lenses feature a "macro mode" function, which allows the lens to be focused much closer than is normally possible, although when set on macro the zoom function of the lens is not available.

Bear in mind that the closer you focus the lens the less the depth of field, and so you may need to set your smallest available aperture. This may result in an extended shutter speed that makes a tripod necessary to avoid camera shake.

△ **By presenting a very selective view** close-ups can be intriguing. Taken from directly above, the top of this substantial metal bollard seems to be on the same plane as the brightly colored webbing lying in a tangle at its base.

△ **The minute depth of field** associated with extreme close-ups can work in the favor of the photographer by reducing the color of the background to a monochromatic blur. As well as subduing intrusive color, the limited depth of field throws the sharply focused section of the blade of grass into the forefront of the frame.

▷ **Picture stories to evoke atmosphere** and a sense of time past often depend on small details. This view into a bookcase with an old calotype portrait among the bound volumes was photographed using a standard lens through smeary glass, which has picked up white and green reflections. These both balance the portrait's gold frame and suggest the faded colors of Victorian gas lamps.

△ **The subtle gradation of color** in this peeling paintwork and rusting wall would probably have passed completely unnoticed if the narrow field of view of the close-up lens had not recorded it in isolation from its surroundings.

◁ **It is only by comparing** the size of the alpine flowers with the softer shapes of the shingle surrounding their stems that we gain any notion of their diminutive size. You have to move in close with subjects as small as this if their color is to have any impact in the final photograph or slide.

▽ **The weathering forces** of rain and sunshine have revealed a history of color preferences stretching back generation after generation. This shed door, which might be regarded as an eyesore in the context of an orderly garden setting, looks like an abstract composition when framed on the page like this.

▷ **To photograph models** in a realistic fashion I prefer to use a 100mm macro lens. A lens of this focal length will give a good-sized image of a small subject, while allowing me to work at some distance. For this shot, the camera was about 3ft (1m) from the toy boat and I jarred the tripod-mounted camera slightly at the moment of exposure to suggest the throbbing of a motor.

◁ **Using extension tubes** greatly extends the range of a lens. In this detail of a Corinthian column, raking sidelight reveals surface texture without producing too much potentially distracting shadow. I stopped down to f22 for maximum depth of field and underexposed by half a stop to improve color saturation.

△ **A simple adaptor** allows you to couple an SLR camera to a micro-scope and admits you to new world of photo-graphic opportunities. This image shows sugar crystals, magnified about 50 times. White light, a mixture of all the colors, was shone through a polarizing filter before reaching the crystals. The emerg-ing light then passed through a second polarizer before reaching the film.

▷ **Frost-covered leaves,** taken with a macro lens at close range, seem to gleam with an inner light. One of the features of this type of close-up is that depth of field is extremely shallow – in this example, only a few centimeters (less than an inch). With such a narrow range of sharp focus, you need to monitor the image on the viewfinder extremely carefully.

Reflected images

An interesting and sometimes utterly surprising way of extending the dimensions of photography is through the use of mirrors or other artificial or naturally occurring reflective surfaces. The surprise when incorporating reflective surfaces within the image area often comes from the parts of a scene they show that are normally hidden from the single fixed eye of the camera. The form of a subject can, thus, be shown from two different angles, often with intriguing changes of color and shape.

Anything is valid to extend the camera's range, and you should be prepared to exploit the distortions, illusions, and juxtapositions produced by polished surfaces, all of which can be used to transform the commonplace world. Since people are accustomed to accepting a lack of definition in reflected images, convincing illusions can be created in mirrors by the use of painted backdrops. Even when taken "straight", mirror images have a degree of mystery that makes them intriguing, especially when they are linked with portraiture.

Make sure that when you are photographing a reflection you focus carefully on the image itself and not simply the surface in which it is seen.

△ **A strange, disembodied portrait** results from using a small hand mirror, hung from a makeshift hook in a canvas wall, to reflect the clown's face, while omitting completely the subject from the frame. This interpretation of the subject could have appeared disturbing had it not been for the expression on his face.

△ **The sloping hillsides** running down to the mirror-calm surface of this mountain lake, as well as the overlapping forms of the more distant hills, can be seen as reflections that are so perfect in both form and coloration that they challenge the substance of the genuine features.

▷ **The slightest ripple** will turn a reflection into a purely abstract design in which colors and shapes are mixed with abandon. The impact of a composition is often strengthened by framing the image so that you cannot see the object casting the reflection.

▽ **Early-morning light** casts attractive yet insubstantial, ghost-like reflections of a harborside skyline onto the placid waters of the bay. Note that the lower the sun is in the sky the more elongated the shadows become.

◁ **The large sheets of glass** used for building panels can be made so that they will distort anything that is reflected in them. Looking out from the inside, however, and the view appears perfectly normal, but, as you can see here, the image of the building opposite has taken on a fluid, almost organic, appearance.

▽ **Looking more like polished bronze** than transparent glass, the selective eye of a telephoto lens has transformed this twilight reflection of a city skyline. Shooting angle is vitally important, determining not only the strength of the reflection but also its precise alignment in the reflective surface.

Color as design

The creative and imaginative possibilities available to the color photographer are just as great – and frequently more stimulating – as the photographer's role of providing a literal record of the world around us.

It is always exciting to explore the way in which common objects and prosaic, unremarkable scenes can be translated into pictures that puzzle the eye and provoke the imagination. The ability to capture the many transformations constantly wrought by the ever-changing intensity and quality of sunlight, by nature, and by chance circumstances depends mainly on the photographer having the desire to look further than simple representation. To make this transition from the mundane to the imaginative, the photographer must learn to "see" the world in a new way, attending to its subjective aspects as well as to the purely compositional elements of line and tone, shape, color, and texture for their own interest and inherent qualities. Once these elements become the subject of photographs, results tend toward the abstract. Camera exposure can have a role to play in this process: underexposure tends to strengthen color saturation, while overexposure has a softening effect on the appearance of color.

△ **Use the camera viewfinder as your window on the world** in order to see what the image will finally look like as a print or transparency. The edging tiles and pool have taken on an intriguingly abstract quality only because the selective view of the camera effectively disguises their true function. What is left is a design relying purely on color for its impact.

▽ **Color has many associations –** the double yellow lines here indicating a stretch of road where parking is prohibited. The humor comes when you see that the lines have been extended down a flight of steps, where cars are not often known to stop.

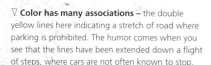

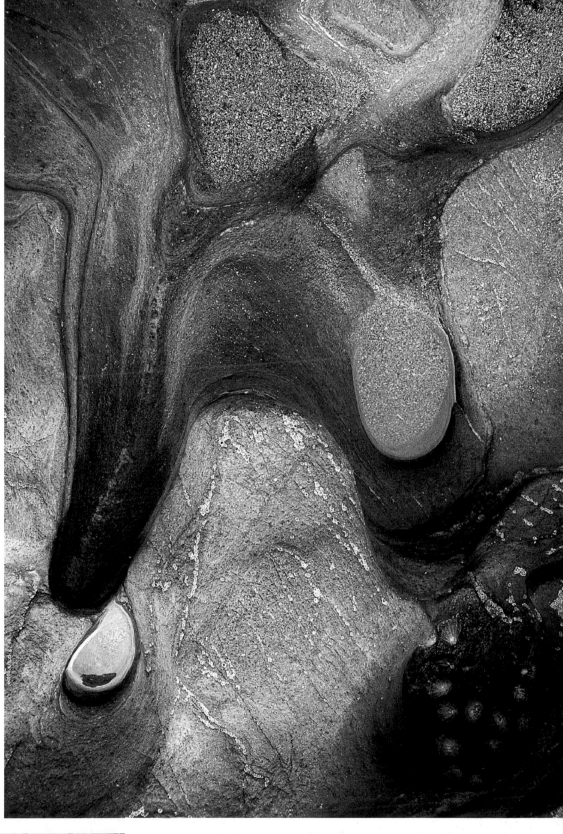

◁ **Bright splashes of color** are provided in this scene through the restaurant owner's random use of mustard yellow, deep orange, and olive green tablecloths. The unifying factors in this color composition are the white top cloths and the regular, triangular shapes of the overlapping material at the ends of the tables.

◁ **Alternating bands** of fully saturated color, where the wooden barn wall is in total shadow, and less saturated color, represented by the thin bands of dappled light, surround a geometrically divided, white-painted window frame. The differences in color weight between the brown and white give the appearance that the frame is floating slightly above the wall.

◁ **Tension is created** in this composition by positioning the parallel lines of wooden decking diagonally within the rectangular shape of the frame. Another strong diagonal is provided by the block of shadow running between top-right and bottom-left corners. In this essentially monochromatic design, tonal variation is paramount.

△ **The tide carves out** a wealth of abstract forms along the shorelines, particularly in soft rock. This eroded area of slate is full of varied colors, forms, and textures, with pools of water, trapped sand and limpet population all contributing to the picture's depth and tonal interest. Note how color intensifies in the more shadowy, slightly underexposed areas of the subject.

Moods of natural light

The sun

The sun, source of natural light and of life itself, is a potent photographic image. Although its sheer energy and intensity make it a difficult subject to handle photographically, its presence never fails to impart vital energy to landscape or seascape pictures, and its hues, varying from white to blood red, may decide the whole balance and mood of a color photograph. If taken straight, in the middle of the day when it is at its most potent, the sun will burn out a picture, causing flare or halation, and may even physically damage a camera's shutter. But there are many ways of avoiding this. By photographing the sun when it is rising or setting, obscured by cloud or haze, shining through translucent material, or half hidden by foreground objects, accurate exposures can be calculated, especially if you use a neutral density or polarizing filter over the lens. Bear in mind, however, that the light intensity changes rapidly at dawn or sunset.

△ **Although not visible,** there is sufficient high-level haze in this picture to scatter some of the wavelengths of light from the sun, giving it an attractive, delicate, pink-tinged rim.

△ **Obscured by cloud,** the sun itself cannot be seen, which helped exposure calculation immensely. This essentially monochromatic skyscape is accented only by an intense highlight edging the topmost surface of the intervening cloud.

▷ **Taking a light reading** directly from a sun-filled sky, even one, like this, that is close to sundown, will give an exposure that will underexpose all objects at ground level. For this shot, I adopted a slightly low camera position to make sure that the distant roof-line would show up as a silhouette against the sky.

◁ **To take this photograph** I pointed the camera at the shoreline, took an exposure reading, locked it into the camera, and then recomposed the shot. In this way, the near water and many of the foreground buildings show sufficient detail, but the sky and sun have completely burned out.

△ **A colored filter** with a clear center spot was used in this example. By framing the composition so that the sun coincided with the clear area of the filter, you can see the effects of both flare and halation.

▽ **Although well above the horizon,** a heavy early-morning mist has reduced the intensity of the sun, confining it to a perfect circular shape. The exposure was too brief to record foreground detail, but the sky has taken on a range of delicate hues all from a restricted part of the spectrum.

◁ **A rush of excited children** charging along a beach, with a background of sky colored deep gold by the setting sun, proved to be perfect foreground elements for this evocative photograph.

△ **Aligning the paddles** of a wind-driven water pump in the Australian outback with the disk of the sun permitted me to set an exposure that did not reduce the landscape to a complete silhouette. An unobscured sun of this intensity could damage your eyes.

▽ **Dust and atmospheric pollution** tend to produce the most dramatic sunset colors, such as this blood-red orb just grazing the horizon. By focusing on the foreground branches, these have been shown sharp in contrast with the slightly soft outline of the sun.

Skies

Although the sun is the ultimate source of natural illumination, the sky, in its infinite variety of atmospheric moods, is the great mediating influence in all out-door photographs. Purely as a background, its colors, varying from blood-red to the palest shades of blue, can determine whether the atmosphere of a picture is calm or turbulent, ominous or happy. As a subject in its own right, it offers a unique range of material as cumulus clouds form and re-form in often enormous sculptural masses, or as cirrus clouds create delicate patterns of light and shade, tone and hue.

In photographing the sky, either as a substantial part of the background or as the main subject, exposure is often a problem, especially if foreground detail is to be included. A bright sky may need up to four stops less exposure than the land it illuminates. If you calculate exposure for the sky alone the foreground will block up into dense shadow with silhouetted features. Exposure calculated for the foreground will show the sky as an area of flat, featureless white. Averaging the two readings does not always solve the problem, although this, coupled with a change of camera angle or field of view of the lens, may considerably help.

△ **Molded by thermal currents,** these clouds seem to have taken on the shape of the landscape over which they float. The play of changing colors and shadows on the ground repeat their patterns. Skyscapes such as this reverse the ratio of two-thirds land to one-third sky usual in landscape photographs.

△ **Drama and impact** in this shot of a sky reflected in a lake have been achieved by exposing only for the sky. This has thrown the land into shadow and silhouetted the cloud patterns against a sinking sun. The use of a wide-angle lens helps to give the feeling of the sky extending over the viewer's head.

△ **A burning sky** dramatizes the dawn, illuminating oak trees on the horizon in silhouette and giving the effect of flames and smoke bursting from the skyline. Photographing effects such as this is not difficult if you expose for the highlights – being in the right place at the right time takes effort.

◁ **The sheen of water** left behind by the retreating waves is sufficiently reflective to pick up the last highlights from the setting sun, not only reflecting colors from the sky but also throwing the underexposed shoreline into sharp, sculpted relief.

△ **Capturing a rainbow on film** is always a little bit special, especially when the setting is as idyllic as this. Rainbows occur when droplets of water in the atmosphere, acting like tiny prisms, split white light into its component colors (see pp. 14–15). No special exposure calculation is necessary – usually, a reading that averages the light levels in a scene is sufficient.

△ **Two aspects of light** are caught in one photograph of crofters' cottages on a remote coast of Scotland. I was standing in autumn sunlight looking toward a cloudburst. Just minutes later the whole sky had blackened. Speed in capturing the vital moment can be as essential in landscape shots as in photojournalism.

▷ **The usual ratio** of land to sky in landscape photographs is 2:1. Here, however, this ratio has been radically altered, and the land – with its small stand of solitary trees balancing the huge bulk of the clouds above – takes up the smallest possible slice at the bottom of the frame. The expansive perspective evident in the picture is the result of using a 24mm wide-angle lens (on a 35mm camera).

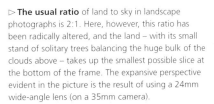

◁ **Rays of sunlight** piercing a gathering storm front at sunset take on an almost ethereal quality, like that seen in tall cathedral buildings when light finds its way inside through high, galleried windows. The highlight reading used for this shot has all but obliterated the farmhouse below through underexposure.

▷ **The glare** from a setting sun is still strong enough to degrade photographic images. Always try, as in this example, to find a camera position where the sun appears hidden behind a cloud.

Water

In outdoor photography, water acts as a powerful yet sensitive mirror of the sky and immediate surroundings, its light and color changing as the sky darkens or clears and its form and shape responsive to winds or currents. Strong light reflected from a body of calm water, especially when seen against dark land masses, can dominate a picture and determine the highlight exposure as well as the mood of the whole scene, which can change according to the angle from which the water is photographed. The sea, which from a height can take on the appearance a sheet of beaten silver, can look turbulent and menacing when photographed from a low angle and against the light.

Rather than being just a part of a landscape scene, water can also provide an effective main subject for a photograph. Not only does water display a marvellous range of hues, from transparent green, through turquoise, to dense blue verging on black, but the spray or mist that rises from the water can transform other colors as it filters the light from the sky. But because water refracts light, the colors of any submerged objects included in the frame tend to be weakened and dissipated.

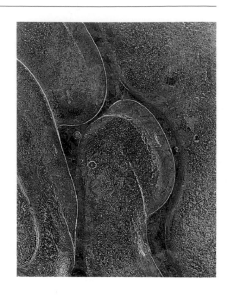

◁ **The dead-calm surface** of an artificial lake acts as a mirror for the heaped masses of cumulus cloud in the sky overhead. The top of a drowned tree becomes an important compositional element by anchoring the eye in the foreground before allowing it to explore the rest of the image.

▷ **Intentional double exposure** in the camera has transformed a rather attractive stretch of water, with its resident swans, into a dream-like image. To achieve this effect, I took one shot with a slight wide-angle and the other with a moderate telephoto lens.

▽ **The turbulent, boiling surf** in this shot was only ankle deep. I photographed the playing figure by shooting into the late afternoon light to turn her into a silhouette and to darken the water. A wide-angle lens and a slow shutter speed helped to give the foreground water its apparent solidity, as well as a depth of field that stretched from a few inches from the camera to the horizon.

◁ **Water comes in many forms,** here as ice. Seen like this, the water has taken on the appearance of sculptured glass, colored by the algae covering the underlying rock

▷ **Moving water** takes on a magical quality when photographed with a very slow shutter speed. Depending on how fast the water is moving, you may need a shutter speed of a second, or even longer, to create this cotton-wool effect. This makes a tripod, or some other stable camera support, vital. I used a shutter speed of 3 full seconds for this photograph. With shutter speeds as long as this, even using your smallest aperture may still result in over-exposure unless you fit a neutral-density filter over the lens.

◁ **Contrast levels** in this seaside scene were so extreme, exposure had to be calculated so that either highlights or shadows would "suffer." The sun was in front of the camera position, although the picture was framed to exclude it, and a highlight reading has reduced the sea walls and figures to the blackest of silhouettes.

Backlighting

The characteristic feature of photography in strong, direct sunlight is the high contrast between areas of deep shade and bright light. Unless light and shade are balanced in an interesting way, results may be disappointing, with harsh sunlight dissipating color and bouncing off reflective surfaces. An alternative is to place the subject between the camera and the sun.

Backlighting (sometimes called *contre-jour*) requires careful judgment of exposure to avoid turning subjects into complete silhouettes, unless that is your intention. Depending on the angle and strength of the light, an allowance of at least two stops will be needed to reveal detail in the shadows. When you are working in very strong sunlight, you may also need to shield the top or sides of the camera to prevent ambient light flaring directly into the lens and degrading results. Screw-in lens hoods are designed to prevent, or minimize, this type of flare, but sometimes you may need to use your free hand as well. If you take these precautions, backlighting or delicate rimlighting enables you to create atmosphere by contrast alone and to take images in soft light that is kinder and more sympathetic to the nature of your subject, especially portrait subjects.

△ **A contrast** of directly lit and backlit palm leaves reveals the intricate designs of nature. The greens would have appeared very solid and uniform had they been photographed in ordinary reflected sunlight. But with the light shining toward the camera through the leaf membrane, all the different densities of hue and layered pattern are shown in well-defined, fan-like shapes.

◁ **Flare is not an issue** when the source of the light is well out of the frame. Bright but weak late-winter sun was the illumination here, and the backlighting is evident in the delicate rim of light outlining the sheep but turning the bare trees into silhouettes.

▽ **If contrast is impossibly high,** decide which extreme of exposure is more important. Here, I took a light reading from the back of my hand, which was largely in shade, and thus set a shutter/ aperture combination that allowed St Michael Mount, Cornwall and the distant hills to record as gray, rather than the black of the immediate foreground, and the water as a shimmering sheet of specular reflections.

▽ **Sunlight bathing the back of the model's head**
had just the right qualities for a softly illuminated,
romantic portrait. Moving in close and taking a light
reading direct from the subject's face gave rise to the
exposure you can see here of ½₀ second at f4. An
averaging light reading of the entire scene, however,
which took in the brightest highlights, indicated an
exposure of ½₀₀ second at f11. Had these settings been
used, all subject detail and color would have turned black.

◁ △ **Color has been
largely sacrificed** in
these scenes of an
indoor horse exercise
session, but what has
been gained is bags of
atmosphere. Sunshine
streaming in through
high windows in one
wall is clearly defined
as tangible shafts of
light by the dust in the
air. For the version on
the left, the lens was
zoomed to the
telephoto end of its
range to pick out just
a few elements of the
general scene above.
In this close-up view, it
is possible to make best
use of the extreme
contrast that existed at
the time of shooting.

Indirect and reflected light

In addition to backlighting (see pp. 88–9), one way of softening the harshness of direct light is to try and position your subjects where they can be illuminated by more delicate light reflected from nearby surfaces, such as garden walls, sides of buildings, windows, and so on. Bear in mind the potential problem of color casts in doing this, however – in general, colorless, white, or neutral-colored surfaces tend to be best. If there are no conveniently positioned nearby surfaces to utilize, the indirect light surrounding a shaded area can often provide adequate illumination and bring out glowing, saturated colors, similar to those seen in diffused or overcast lighting conditions.

 If your subject can be repositioned, try moving into direct shade and then use a portable reflector (which could be as simple as a piece of white cardboard) to bounce a little light into the frame. Likewise, portable accessory flash can also be brought into play as an indirect light source – if you can use it off-camera. Sometimes, pointing the flash head at the floor at your subject's feet will produce just enough reflected illumination to bring out a peron's or object's full color potential, without overpowering the mood of the natural light.

△ **Bright but diffused** light reflecting from the wall behind this curious little girl shows the interior of the shop as well as the reflections in the glass. The colors were subdued by the shadowless light, but because of the white surfaces I took a meter reading from my hand to make sure skin tones were accurate.

△ **When the sun is the correct position** inside light levels can be very high, as in this church interior. By moving the camera position to the back of the church and shooting toward the brightly lit area behind the pulpit, most of the decorated surfaces are shown by softer, indirect light.

▷ **Lightly overcast skies** were responsible for this fully descriptive yet gentle lighting effect. Although there was plenty of light for the photograph, all of it was filtered by the thin clouds before reaching the farmyard where the sheep were being mustered.

▽ **Reflective surfaces,** such as the dark-glazed plate and the skins of these autumn fruits, are destroyed by direct lighting. Here I used reflected studio flash, allowing a carefully positioned corner of direct light to reach the rim of the plate.

◁ **Interior light levels** were too low to produce a satisfactory exposure for both the figure and the background. To overcome this problem, a small accessory flash was used, but its head was pointed at the ground half way between the camera and the subject's feet. This reflected back enough light to lift the illumination on the face by just the right amount.

▽ **A heavy downpour** was sweeping through the city streets when this photograph was taken. At the far end of the road, clouds had parted enough to allow some sunlight through, but the part of the scene with the walking figure was lit solely by light filtering through rain clouds. Note how this illumination has brought out the depth of color in the man's umbrella and on the blurred colors of the speeding bus.

Diffused light

Under overcast skies, the world becomes more enclosed and intimate, and subtleties of tone and color begin to appear that would be swamped under brighter, more direct lighting conditions. Diffused lighting occurs outdoors most often when sunlight is filtered through cloud or is bounced off water moisture, dust, smoke or other minute particles suspended in the atmosphere before it reaches ground level. These conditions tend to scatter the available light in all directions, reducing the intensities of both shadows and highlights and, thus, lowering image contrast.

In the studio, the simplest way to replicate this type of diffused lighting is by fitting a soft box over the lighting head. A soft box is a lightweight pyramidal frame covered with heavy-duty plastic. The base of the pyramid, through which the flash shines to reach the subject, is made from white-colored translucent plastic that thoroughly mixes and diffuses the light, and takes away the clinical harshness that is so often associated with flash illumination.

Indoors or out, another way to achieve the qualities of diffused lighting is to position a sheet of finely textured glass between the light source and subject.

▷ **A diffusing filter** and a moderately wide aperture of f4 on a short telephoto lens has softened this close-up view of a meadow in full flower. The limited depth of field has helped to foreshorten perspective in the scene and this, linked with a very low camera position, produces a child-like fantasy view of the world.

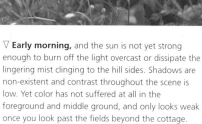

▽ **Early morning,** and the sun is not yet strong enough to burn off the light overcast or dissipate the lingering mist clinging to the hill sides. Shadows are non-existent and contrast throughout the scene is low. Yet color has not suffered at all in the foreground and middle ground, and only looks weak once you look past the fields beyond the cottage.

△ **A rain-splattered window** acts as an effective diffuser in this image of a flower display in a large ornamental bowl. Diffusers are normally employed between the light source and subject, not subject and camera, so here image degradation is noticeable but the effect is striking.

△ **Cloud cover** was too solid for sunset colors to appear in the sky, and down in the valleys between the towering buildings it is already dark enough for street lights, window displays, and car headlights to contribute their multicolored highlights. Although only a few minutes of daylight were left when this shot was taken, detail has not been lost anywhere in the frame, and colors remain sharp and well-defined.

◁ **A soft landscape** full of subtle shades and delicate colors becoming progressively lighter as the distance from the camera increases. This quality was not the result of any trick of the light, however, but was due to a film of fine dust that was kicked up into the atmosphere earlier that morning after strong winds had blown through the region.

Early morning

The freshness and delicacy of early morning light, with its gradual deepening of pearly colors, is unlike any other. Minute by minute, a world composed entirely of tones of gray, while the disk of the sun is still below the horizon, becomes tinted until colors intensify and glow, even in the angular shadows, as the sun climbs higher and higher into the sky. As temperatures rise, frost melts, dew evaporates, and the air dries.

From a photographic viewpoint, another feature that is often noticeable in the early morning is the clarity of the light. While the world beneath is largely still, traffic is sporadic, and other forms of human activity is in a temporary lull, the atmosphere's burden of paticulates is at its lowest.

Bear in mind that early morning light is fragile, and levels overall will be low. A suitably fast film will thus be necessary if you are to avoid having to support your camera to prevent the effects of camera shake. But the light changes rapidly at this time of day, and if you have a high vantage point you can watch as the shadows retreat across the landscape. If you are setting camera controls manually, monitor your light meter constantly to avoid exposure errors.

▷ **Just after sunrise** and the landscape is devoid of human activity. At this quiet time of day you can find a clarity of lighting that looks unnaturally sharp. Each band of color in this agricultural scene is clearly demarcated, as are the still-dense shadows cast by the more prominent features in the terrain.

△ **A localized sheet of high cloud** greets the rising sun climbing over an alpine snow field. Until the sun climbs higher in the sky and swings around, the surrounding mountains will remain backlit and retain their steely blue color, which contrasts starkly with snow below and conjures up the icy coldness of early morning. The snow, still criss-crossed with yesterday's ski tracks, has a crusty film of ice preventing any powder snow being kicked up by the early skiers.

▷ **Delicate subtleties** of color and tone have all been preserved in this landscape, showing a community of farm workers taking advantage of the first rays of dawn to finish gathering in the harvest.

◁ **Overnight frost,** briefly preserved by the bars of a farm gate, has given substance to shadows in a picture that is almost an abstraction of dawn. The low sun directly behind the camera position casts eerily long shadows, which, because of the pattern of frost, show clearly my shadow behind the gate as I took the picture.

▷ **The lagoon** feeding the famous canals of Venice is already well lit in this early morning photograph, but the gondolas moored opposite in the immediate foreground of the picture are still in deep shade. It is the contrast between highlight and shadow, color and tone that has created such a compelling composition.

△ **Early morning** is a time of preparation – of exercising horses, hosing them down, and grooming them. Frail sunlight penetrates the mist, but the heavily coated soldiers, frosty park, and pools of water all convey the exhilarating coolness of the hour following the dawn. The atmosphere breathed out by this picture is the result partly of autumnal light and color and partly of the subject matter itself.

Midday

At noon the light of the sun is whiter than at any other time of the day. If the atmosphere is clear, without heat haze, and if the strength of the light does not dissipate colors through glare, hues are at their brightest with the contrast between them sharp. Tonal contrasts are even more marked, with intense highlights and short, deep shadows. In summer, with the sun more directly overhead, the angle of the light tends to obscure form and emphasize pattern, making portraiture particularly difficult. Faces may be hidden in the shade and eyes are usually lost in deep shadow.

If you are photographing in intense light and cannot avoid it by positioning your subject against the light or in shadow, slow film will make it easier to control exposure. Ultraviolet, neutral density, and polarizing filters will help to reduce haze, brightness, and glare, and a yellow filter may sometimes be useful for color accuracy if indirect light from an intense blue sky is likely to produce a blue cast. There are times, however, when the harsh quality of midday light in summer should not be avoided but rather used for its dramatic effects. Pictures containing high contrasts of light and shade may produce striking and evocative imagery.

△ **Time of day** is not the only regulator of lighting quality, as this photograph demonstrates. Although taken just after noon, a large patch of isolated cloud moved in front of the sun just as the shutter was tripped. The intense brightness of the colors disappeared almost at once, but this was replaced by well-saturated hues and a distinct lessening of subject contrasts.

△ **When the light of midday** is so intense colors are likely to be weak and dissipated, move your subject into the shade, if possible. That was the solution in this instance, especially when I noticed the distinct pink coloration of the stone-flagged verandah. I made sure that enough of the beach could be seen through the archway against which the subject was leaning.

▷ **Depending on their orientation to the sun,** surfaces photographed in bright light from a clear sky at midday tend to be either brightly lit or deeply shadowed. This would not be such a potential exposure problem – such contrasts are nearly always beyond the recording capability of your film – if the shadows and highlights were not adjacent to each other. Here, the exposure reading was taken from the highlights and the deeper shadows were allowed to block up completely.

▷ **Noonday sun,** which was the lighting used for this picture taken in Luxor, Egypt, produces a starkness devoid of subtle shading of tone or color. Shadows should, therefore, be regarded as an essential compositional device and be exploited for their capacity to set the mood for a picture.

△ **In the temperate regions of the world,** taking pictures when the sun is directly overhead does not bring with it the same problems you would encounter in hotter locations. However, the lighting intensity can still bring out every ounce of brightness in a landscape, especially in this coastal scene in which the white chalk cliffs appear stark against their dark green, grass-covered tops.

▽ **It was about an hour** before midday and the air was already throbbing with heat when I took this picture. Everything and everybody moved slowly to conserve energy, and this photograph composed, uncompromisingly, of lit and unlit surfaces seems to express perfectly the atmosphere at the time.

Dusk and night

Even after a solidly overcast day, skies tend to clear toward evening. Clouds, especially near the horizon, often break up, giving rise to beautifully diffused light tinged with gold if the sun is still setting or with blue as the night draws on. Early evening is the ideal time to take pictures that give the impression of night. In total darkness, highlights tend to be harsh, with spreading areas of halation surrounding light sources, and shadows displaying no detail at all.

To cope with the conditions you will encounter at dusk, a camera with a fast lens (f1.2–f2.8) is essential of you want to avoid slow shutter speeds. For speeds slower than ⅓₀ second a tripod, or some other support, will be necessary. If there are any artificial light sources in the picture, perhaps from street lights or illuminated windows, you will need to make a choice between daylight- and tungsten-balanced film, depending on the color result you want.

For photographs of wildlife, dusk is often the best time to go hunting, since this is when nocturnal animals start to become active. In the dimmer light, they feel safe and confident. It is always a good idea to carry a pencil torch so that you can see to make any necessary camera adjustments.

△ **You have to work quickly** when photographing around dusk. At this time of day, light levels dip second by second, and color tints and highlights can fade and then vanish before you are able to react. A strong foreground feature, even if underexposed, helps to balance compositions of the night sky.

△ **The moon** in this landscape had risen while there was still plenty of twilight left. Had night descended fully, the 2-second exposure needed for the moon would have left the remainder of the frame black and lacking in detail.

◁ **Because they can be so colorful** it may be tempting to shoot sunsets with nothing else of interest in the frame. However, a strong subject element, such as these gum trees, may give your shot more interest.

◁ **Not all sunsets** produce a dramatically colorful display. In this case, the empty canvas presented by the flat area of wet sand, water, and sky proved to be perfect for the use of a colored special-effects filter. This filter has an even, overall color, although others are available that graduate in strength from top to bottom, and others that have a clear central area.

△ **Early evening** is one of the best times to take photographs when you want full color saturation without sacrificing subject detail. The slanting, form-revealing light coming from a low sun shows architectural subjects to good advantage if you adopt the appropriate camera position.

◁ **In a sheltered bay** such as this, you will often find that at least one of surrounding hillsides directly faces the setting sun. If the light reflecting back from its sun-lit face then becomes trapped, exposure within the bay can be very consistent.

Spring

Perhaps it is the sheer contrast with the grayness of winter, with its low, overcast skies, bare trees, and gloomy afternoons, that the light and the colors of spring seem so vibrant and alive, and certainly fresher than those of any other season. The countryside reawakens in a gentle explosion of new foliage and grass, early flowers, sprouting shrubs, buds, and blossoms. The photographs everybody likes to take of fledgling birds or wobbly legged animals are given a sparkling quality by the clear, angular light, and candid shots of people outdoors in spring weather tend to be characteristically relaxed and cheerful.

Another feature of the spring season is its weather. Although it comes as a longed-for relief after the winter months, spring is often an unsettled time of year. Sudden spring showers can heighten the colors of nature, but they are often unexpected and violent enough to destroy delicate blossoms and send animals and birds running for cover. If you come across a likely subject, take the first available opportunity to grab your shot if the conditions look like they may be about to change. Early morning is a good time for pictures – especially when the buds have just opened after a calm night and are still damp with dew.

△ **The transition between seasons** is evident in this wood. The fresh green of spring's new leaves are not yet dense enough to disguise the skeletal, winter shapes of the trees, and on the ground the leaf litter from the previous autumn has not yet been fully incorporated into the soil.

△ **Flower-filled meadows** in the dappled light cast by trees not yet with the complete heads of foliage that will restrict light at ground level later in the season, are becoming an increasingly rare sight. The general move to monoculture, practiced in enormous fields sometimes stretching from horizon to horizon, sweeps away so much beauty in the relentless march toward economy of scale.

▷ **Spring blossoms** are usually individually quite small, relying for their impact on the sheer number of flowers. A general picture of an orchard of blossom trees can make a wonderful image, but so too can close-ups of the individual blooms. Only by moving in close can you truly appreciate the subtlety of their coloring and form. A lens with a macro setting is useful for pictures such as these.

◁ **As soon as winter frosts have past** many birds turn their attentions to nest building. If you are familiar with the habits of the birdlife in your region you will have a head start in recording pictures such as this nest with its clutch of six speckled eggs. Fringed with tall, water-growing reeds, you would never find a nest like this unless you knew where to look.

▽ **The gentle light** of early spring – filtered yellow by the still translucent leaves that have only recently opened – falls on the nodding heads of a bluebell carpet. Notice how color saturation increases in the more shadowy areas and color brightness in the highlights. Framing your shot to include both types of area, highlights and shadows, makes a visually more complex image that is likely to attract and then hold the viewer's attention.

Summer

The months of summer are the most popular of all for photography. This, after all, is the traditional time for taking family vacations, and many people take the majority of their pictures during those few weeks while on vacation. Yet the intense light of summer is often the most difficult to handle, especially at midday, when forms can be obscured by heavy shadows and colors are often masked by glare from reflective surfaces. Backlighting and indirect lighting can be effectively used to reduce the level of contrast on the subject or provide a softer light for portraits. Another strategy is to avoid the harsh, uncompromising light of full day altogether and exploit instead the gentle light of early morning or long evenings when people are more relaxed and the rich colors of nature are seen to the greatest advantage. Particularly after rain, green grass will look greener and blue skies bluer than at any other time. Shooting in the cooler part of the day will also reduce the problems of sun flaring in to the camera lens or heat affecting exposed films. When you are going on vacation, avoid the temptation to load yourself up with exhausting extra equipment. One camera body and three lenses (or two zooms) will cover most eventualities.

△ **The sun-dappled street** in this photograph suggests coolness, although it was photographed in the oppressive heat of a Bombay summer. Notice how the reflected light illuminates the intricate façade of the tenement block, bringing out all its subtlety of color and helping to accentuate form.

◁ **A prominent foreground feature** and sidelighting to bring out the texture and form of the circular hay bale, have combined to produce this image of summer. Take away the bale and the large expanse of stubble would dominate, and the impact of the scene would evaporate.

▽ **A radically different perspective** produces a new view of a familiar type of scene, one that allows us to appreciate the unconscious pattern and design of farming activity on the country-side. This image was taken from a few hundred feet off the ground in the basket of a hot-air balloon.

△ **The intensity of summer light** on the Indonesian island of Bali has robbed the scene of the saturated green hues we normally associate with that tropical location. But instead we see the undulating shapes of the rice terraces with greater clarity, each topped with water so still and reflective that it appears almost solid.

△ **There is no "wrong" lighting.** The harshness of the landscape in the part of the Australian outback where this photograph was taken was ideally suited to the blindingly bright light of the summer sun, which has brought out all the color of the iron-oxide-bearing rocks.

▽ **The famous hall of pillars** in the Temple of Karnak, Luxor, is nearly always illuminated by a high sun, but form and texture are more obvious features in the shadows, while shape becomes paramount in the areas recorded in bright light.

▷ **A ferry on the Bosporus** leaves behind a sun-drenched Istanbul. The clouds building up to a summer storm are important compositional elements here, and so the scene was framed accordingly.

△ **Ultraviolet light** is not an uncommon factor in coastal scenes. The haze-like conditions it creates dissipates strong colors, as you can see in the distant water, making the colors in the immediate foreground appear stronger in comparison.

Autumn

The annual transition from ripeness to decay that occurs in autumn provides marvellous opportunities for color photography, not only of broad landscape scenes but also of close-ups of telling details. Increasingly, toward winter, the weather becomes turbulent with strong winds, dense clouds, the first frosts, and damp mists. Days shorten, while the light itself grows slightly redder than in summer, and because of its height and position in the sky the sun casts longer shadows, describing more searchingly forms, textures, and colors. As the foliage of the trees turns from full greens to vivid reds and golds, and as the winds begin to expose the sculptural forms of the landscape, color contrasts are at their most dramatic and glowing.

The best time to take advantage of the uniquely soft light of autumn is in the early morning and late afternoon; and the full richness of the season's colors is effectively photographed not only in isolation but also against the darker greens of pastures of evergreen trees or the sober hues of bare soil. If the weather starts to look inclement, rather than heading indoors for shelter, turn the camera on those cloud-laden skies and trees bent in supplication to the wind.

△ **This brilliant autumn scene** in Vermont is given additional interest for the viewer and a sense of scale by the inclusion of subject elements of known size we can identify with – the man and his dog. The darker green of the background trees acts as an effective contrast to the reds and oranges of the nearer trees.

▷ **An old, established** ivy vine supported by the trunk of the foreground tree produces an effect of fully leafed branches that is at odds with the evidence of autumn lying all about on the ground. Caught in a beam of bright yet gentle sunlight, the yellow of the leaf litter seems to glow out of the frame.

△ **The bare soil and brown foliage** speaks to us of autumn and the color acts as the perfect foil for the leaves touched by the yellow of decay. As the clouds above the camera position become increasingly dense and threatening, the atmosphere of the image becomes confined and claustrophobic, relieved only by the distant background of hills that are still free of cloud and bathed in silver-colored light.

▷ **Many cultivated plants,** such as this delicately colored rose, have had their flowering season extended well into the autumn. If you select the right subject you can take close-ups with the type of lens the averagely equipped photographer will own, but make sure the background is well enough out of focus not to compete for attention.

△ **Soft but powerful angular light** sweeps across an autumnal wood to reveal the complex strength of a beech tree. Thinning leaves have let the light of a midday sun penetrate the entire scene, so that individual forms and colors can be seen clearly, and a delicate interplay of light and shade contrasts with the bold image of the tree.

▷ **Cold nights and fine, hazy days** produce the brilliant tints and sharp contrasts of foliage seen in this lakeside forest. A low angle of light gives sheen to the water, accentuating the thrust of the bank of tall trees, their colors varying from dark green to gray, pink, yellow and orange.

Winter

Rain, sleet, snow, and fog – images of winter – suggest diminished light and muted colors. Yet on a fine winter's day that air has a cold, rinsed freshness that gives colors a particular clarity.

As the hours of daylight lessen, the effects of changing light tend to be condensed. A winter's afternoon can give a low, orange-tinted light similar to that of a summer's evening, emphasizing textures and revealing surprising colors. In a snow-covered landscape, nature's outlines tend to soften, land and sky merging. But the shapes of man-made things are often accentuated, buildings standing out more blackly and boldly against snow or pale skies. As colors are subdued, tone and pattern become more important elements in the overall composition.

The moods of winter light can be discovered by recording the imagery of winter – bare trees, frozen water, cobwebs sparkling with frost, the crystalline fur of snow on a window ledge, glowing fires, and the bright woollens of people muffled in gloves and scarves. Apart from the contrasts of colors against snow, delicate tints often appear, especially in the early morning or toward evening when the light is often a soft pink or orange.

△ **Spiky peaks of frost** clinging to exposed winter berries speak of freezing overnight conditions. Unless daytime temperatures don't rise above freezing, the best time of day for shots like this is mid-morning, when the sun is well above the horizon but the air is still fully chilled.

△ **A light dusting of snow** lies on the ground, and there is a promise of more to come in the heavy sky. In such weather conditions, what little available light there is can be become sealed in between land and sky.

◁ **The way in which you interpret exposure** depends on the type of result you want. Here, I took an exposure reading directly from the brightly lit snow, knowing full well that this would underexpose the horse and riders.

◁ **Heavily diffused light,** caused by mist and snow flurries, for example, can help to even out light levels in a snow scene, making exposure more consistent overall. However, you must then expect colors to be less saturated than they would be in direct and indirect sunlight.

◁ **A mountain snow field** is seen here, washed with bright sunlight coming from a sky so clear you feel as if you can see for ever. This amount of snow acts as a giant reflector and will fool your meter into selecting a small aperture and/or a fast shutter speed, leading to underexposure of anything seen against it.

△ **Snow in this scene** has obliterated most signs of modern times, making this old mill appear as if it is a snapshot from some previous age. More recent structures on the left of the frame have been cleverly hidden by the bare trees in the foreground, which, together with the branches intruding on the right, make the perfect frame for the building.

△ **What would appear as leaf litter** in the autumn waiting to be swept up and removed has been transformed by a light coating of ice. Use your camera's viewfinder carefully, looking at all four corners, to make sure that everything that will be included in the photograph is making a positive contribution to the composition.

▷ **A desolate country road** running to the skyline appears to be spotlit by the white rim of the setting sun. In fact, the sun had already gone down below the horizon, and the illusion of sunlight is provided by the headlights of an on-coming car.

▽ **Daylight from a weak sun** filtering through a thin veil of high cloud has reduced contrast generally within this scene, but especially on the building, which appears isolated and somewhat desolate in its winter landscape.

△ **The clarity of light** in winter can be something very special, so don't put your camera away just because it is cold outside. These highland cows in Scotland stood transfixed in a sunbeam, soaking up every once of warmth, and moving only as the sun shifted its position.

◁ **Details can be as evocative** as broad landscape scenes. Crystals of ice still clinging to the tops of this wrought-iron fence and coating the strands of a spider's web, says all that is necessary about the winter season. Just a few minutes after this shot was taken, the steadily warming air had turned the ice to water.

▽ **Tussocks of rough grass** are all that have survived in the frozen ground of this Scottish highland scene. The skies were clear, however, and the watery sunshine touching the isolated crofter's cottage and outbuildings brought with it a warming, rosy light.

Shooting in poor light

Poor light can be anything from fog or rain to failing light. As light dims, color values tend to darken and blend together and, at this point, many photographers put their equipment away. Yet there is no such thing as bad light for photography. Next time you are out in the open in a gathering storm, look carefully at the scene around you and notice how different objects appear. If there is a dark cloud base, the sky will have sealed in the available light producing rich color saturation despite the dulling of more brilliant hues.

Successful photography in most types of poor light is more a matter of patience, experience, and alertness than of special equipment. Basically, you need a lightweight, easily handled SLR or compact that, in rain, you can keep under your coat until the last possible moment. Fast film – around ISO 1600 – and a lens with a wide maximum aperture – say f2.8 or larger – will also be of great help in exploiting every last bit of available light. If depth of field is important and you want to use a smaller aperture, then the resulting shutter speed may require you to use a tripod to avoid camera shake. Bear in mind that poor light will in general help you to balance your picture by reducing contrasts of light and shade.

△ **Dimly lit interiors** present problems, but over-lighting may destroy the atmosphere. Here, I exposed for the weak light on the face of the reclining Buddha and monk, bracing myself against a wall for ¼-second exposure at f2.8 using ISO 200 film.

◁ **Heavy cloud cover** that casts part of a scene into deep shadow while other parts remain in bright sunshine can pose problems. Taking an exposure reading from the shadows in this example would have so massively overexposed the sky that there simply was no option other than to take a light reading from the highlights.

▽ **Muted colors** often result when pictures are taken under heavily overcast skies, as you can see in this photograph of a shepherd's bad-weather shelter standing out against the exposed clay of the surrounding high hills.

▷ **Color casts** can occur unexpectedly. Dusk was beginning to gather when this picture was taken, and the sun was in the opposite part of the sky. Thus, the only light illuminating the scene was that from a blue sky. Note how strongly the shiny tin roof of the cottage has taken up this color. The other color cast is what you would expect – an overly warm glow from a domestic tungsten light recorded on daylight-balanced film.

◁ **The sun had already set** when this picture of a ramshackle village by a river in Thailand was taken. Under a sunless sky, all colors are well saturated but they have been dulled and lost much of their vibrancy and brilliance. Detail, however, is pin-sharp throughout the image.

▷ **Shooting in poor light** is a problem commonly encountered by wildlife photographers, since their subjects rarely oblige by posing in bright sunlight. For this shot of a tiger in a zoo in Singapore, light rain was falling and light levels were so poor I underexposed the shot to avoid using a shutter speed that would have inevitably produced camera shake. To compensate, I pushed the film two stops in processing.

Fog and mist

Moisture in the air, even when you cannot see it, diffuses light to some degree, but once it becomes visible it poses special problems for the photographer. These, however, can be overcome to give pictures that are full of interest and atmosphere. The quality of light on misty or foggy days tends to be biased toward blue if conditions are totally overcast, or red if there is any visible morning or evening sun. The pale, fragile light reduces depth and form in the scene, increasing the tendency toward two-dimensional flatness in pictures. Colors and contrasts are softened alike, and because the light is scattered scenes can have a duality of tone from light distance to darker foreground.

In order to capture the mist itself you need to expose for the highlights. Slight overexposure will enable you to penetrate the fog, but it is easy to miscalculate. Bear in mind that any available light there is will be bounced around within the droplets of moisture making up the mist or fog, and your light meter can be misled into reading more light than there in fact is. To be safe, take a close-up light reading from your hand in the light and then overexpose by about half a stop. Keep your camera and lens protected from wet fog when it is not in use.

△ **A highlight reading** has reduced the figure here to little more than a silhouette. But given the size of the figure in the overall scene, it would have been inappropriate to have made an exposure allowance.

▷ **Fog often lingers** near bodies of water, even when the sun has burned it off in adjacent areas. When the diffusing effect of fog reduces the color content of a scene, it is interesting to note how important shape becomes to compensate.

▽ **When the sky is predominantly overcast,** the color bias in a resulting photograph tends toward blue, as you can see in this fog-shrouded valley. As a result, the effects of aerial perspective become exaggerated, increasing the sense of distance.

▽ **Fog effects** can be added as a darkroom effect. To produce the image here, a sheet of lightweight tracing paper was intermittently inserted into the enlarger light beam so that the bottom two-thirds of the print was mostly affected.

◁ **A steadily strengthening sun** had already restored the full range of colors to the near bank, and the river mist was rapidly dissipating when this shot was taken. The increasing warmth of the day is reflected in the generally warm glow throughout the scene.

◁ **Rising mist on a warm morning** in early autumn dissipates the vivid colors of the trees along a river bank as a rowing crew glide by in training. A low shooting angle emphasizes the foreground reeds standing proud of the water, and helps to give the impression of the sleek boat slicing easily through the tranquil water.

△ **A high camera angle** looking down on fog banks in the valleys below gives an image that is full of mystery and atmosphere. Fog tends to collect around streams and rivers as well as in gullies where the land is lowest, and the sun often needs to be high in the sky before this atmospheric moisture is burned off.

Rain and storms

Falling rain can impart a strong atmosphere to photographs, often with beautiful, subdued hues. If your camera becomes wet, then you will need to dry it as soon as possible to prevent potential damage, and never handle film when your hands are wet. To protect the lens from moisture, screw a clear-glass or UV filter into the front mount. Any water on the front element of the lens (or on a filter) will soften the image, so constantly check for this and dry it as necessary.

Startling, distorted, and often intense hues appear under storm conditions, when heavy cloud cover refracts certain colors, often producing an eerie greenish light. A variety of atmospheric effects – clouds, wind, rain, snow, lightning, hail, and shafts of unexpected sun – transforms the appearance of the world as light changes rapidly in quality and intensity. Summer storms are especially exciting when strong sun, rain clouds, and wind all combine to alter the light, seemingly by the second. To capture the turbulence of a scene, expose for the highlights so that the areas in shadow are left dark, thus giving a full range of contrasts. Including the source of the light in the picture will add to its mood and impact, as will wet roads, swaying trees, and people scurrying for cover.

△ **Already too wet to make any difference,** this rain-soaked pedestrian has abandoned any attempt to shelter from a sudden summer downpour. Illuminated from the rear, a shaft of sunshine has transformed her black hair, turning it into a rim of white, and each individual droplet of water suspended in the air seems to glow with an inner radiance.

▷ **Looking upward with the camera** emphasizes the vulnerability of a young tree, as the power of a storm slowly builds in the sky above it. Without the tonal contrast provided by the light-colored bark of the foreground tree and the dark tones of all else in the scene, the photograph would have looked flat and two-dimensional.

▷ **An ordinary patch of tarmac road** has been transformed into a fascinating pattern of circles forming and re-forming in heavy rain. The shallow puddle of water produces a good contrast of light and shade, and by using a fast shutter speed of $\frac{1}{500}$ second it was possible to record clearly the radiating ripples.

◁ **Unless rain is very heavy** it tends to disappear when it is photographed. When this picture was taken the air was saturated with fine mist, but the only visible effect of this is a general muting of the landscape colors.

◁ **After the storm front** has passed by, the air is scrubbed clean of the minute particles of dust, smoke, and pollutants that diffuse and soften the effects of sunlight. Pictures taken at this time can show a purity of color and a sharpness of detail that are difficult to reproduce in any other circumstances.

△ **The intensity and clarity** of pre-storm light can sometimes be overpowering, almost beyond the ability of film emulsion to capture fully. In this example, the ominously dark cloud cover allowed a single port-hole of light through to the land below. Caught in this natural spotlight, the farmhouse and outbuildings are bathed in a rosy glow that you know will be snuffed out by a thunderous bang any second.

Snow and cold

Apart from the purely practical difficulties of simply keeping warm and the discomfort of handling equipment or changing films with numbed fingers, photography in the snow raises several special problems. Perspective and other normal guidelines often vanish, making it difficult to judge size, distance, or height. The even quality of the available light and the lack of tonal recession tend to flatten landscapes. Strong blue casts appear in shadows, especially under overcast skies just before a snowfall, or in area of settled snow illuminated by a an intensely blue sky. Under bright skies, the intensity of the light also produces meter readings that are too high, leading to underexposure of most things seen against the snow.

   Although experience will help you to overcome these problems, the best way of adapting to snowy conditions is to take pictures that exploit the beauty of the monochromatic tones and patterns. Falling snow should be photographed at fairly slow shutter speeds to show streaks or at fast speeds to arrest individual flakes. Bear in mind that as the temperature falls your camera batteries become less efficient and will need changing more often.

△ **Shooting from a camera angle** that shows bare earth in the foreground and a snowy scene beyond is one way to overcome the problem of a lack of tonal recession making winter landscapes look flat in photographs.

▷ **The dark upper storey** of the lodge and the elongated shadow cast by a late-afternoon sun are vital components in this landscape, since they provide the type of tonal contrast that is often missing in snow scenes.

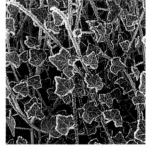

△ **Details can be just as telling** as a broader landscape scene. By rising early in the morning, before the sun has had a chance to warm the air, it is possible to record images of frost still fringing such hardy evergreen plants as this ivy, which now looks as if it is a variegated variety.

▷ **Coated in small snow crystals,** these fractured plywood boards look like like they are victims of the severe weather. The color of the boards varies considerably, depending on the thickness of snow on top.

△ **The contrast** between the dark-toned plants in
the immediate foreground and the flat white of the
snow field beyond helps to restore some of the
perspective in this photograph. Using subjects close
to the camera like this also help to distract from what
is a rather empty middle ground.

◁ **Color can be so subdued** by even the lightest
covering of snow, that you need to think more like
a black and white photographer than a color one,
taking more account of tone than hue, and shape
than color. And the placement of subject elements
becomes even more crucial than normal since there
is less to distract the eye. Note here how the single
tree in the middle ground balances the copse of trees
in the background, for example.

▽ **Using a zoom lens** I was able to frame this
steeply sloping hillside without changing camera
position to exclude the part of the snow field directly
in front of me that had been marred by footprints
and ski tracks.

Heat

Color photography in extreme heat is often affected by blinding glare, either direct from the sun or reflected from nearby shiny surfaces, haze, and dust, all of which tend to dissipate color. A neutral density filter (available in different strengths) will cut down the amount of light reaching the film without upsetting the tonal or color balance of a scene. As a general guide, you should underexpose by half to two-thirds of an stop in order to increase color saturation.

Most of the problems presented by hot climates are purely mechanical ones. To prevent sand or dust working their way into your camera and jamming the shutter or scratching the film, you should inspect and carefully clean your camera and lenses each evening. An ultraviolet (UV) filter can be left permanently on the lens to protect the delicate front element from abrasion, dust, finger marks, and so on. Protect spare lenses in a sealable plastic bag inside a proper camera case. If high humidity is also a factor, keep a few small bags of silica gel inside the case to absorb moisture. Condensation may form on your camera equipment if you take it out of an air-conditioned room on a hot day. Counter this by leaving equipment outdoors in the shade for half an hour before use.

△ **Skies bleached of all color** can be a problem in very hot climates. To add interest to the sky in this picture, which was a featureless area of white at the top of the frame, a tobacco-colored half-filter was used over the camera lens. When using filters such as this, twist it around on the lens so that the color aligns with a white or light-toned part of the image.

△ ▷ **A muster of the local wild horses** is an annual event in parts of the Australian interior. To prevent undue stress to the horses, both wild and saddle (and the riders), this activity starts at sun up, before the heat can build up into a throbbing intensity impossible to work in. The powder-dry dust kicked up by the horses in both these pictures helps to communicate the atmosphere of the scene.

◁ **Slight underexposure** has restored some of the intensity of color of this sun-dried field in Greece, with its ranks of olive trees and scattered patches of wild flowers taking advantage of the transitory shade they cast.

△ **An adobe settlement** looms up on a high escarpment, the color of its baked-clay exterior almost the same as that of the sun-hardened courtyard in front of it.

◁ **Each figure** in this South American market scene is surrounded by the smallest possible puddle of shadow, indicating the sun was directly overhead, and at its hottest, when this photograph was taken.

▽ **A different angle** on a familiar landmark – Ayers Rock. Here, the heat of the day has been made clear to the viewer by the choice of a camera position that allows flare from direct sunshine to enter part of the lens. This technique needs to be handled with restraint if the subject matter is not to be subverted.

Using artificial light

Tungsten and daylight

In the early morning and evening colors are either emerging from the night or ebbing into it, and the "truth" of a particular hue is completely subjective. If there is any source of artificial light, the situation becomes even more complex and the colors of a scene will depend to a large extent on your choice of film – daylight balanced or tungsten balanced.

The most beautiful effects are achieved when one source of light predominates, with just a touch of the other. Usually, the principal light source in a scene will dictate your choice of film. If, for example, an evening sky retains a lot of light while a few house lights are beginning to wink on, you will probably choose daylight film, and the effect will be to make the house lights look a warm orange color. Daylight film used to photograph tungsten light strengthens reds and yellows in a scene and gives whites an orange cast. Conversely, tungsten film used to photograph daylight brings up the blues, subdues reds and yellows, and gives a bluish cast to whites. In full daylight, this produces an eerie, unnatural atmosphere. Tungsten film can sometimes be used effectively at sunset, turning reddish skies a dramatic magenta. But unless your intention is to create a special effect, it is best to match your film to suit the predominant light source.

△ **When tungsten and daylight** appears in the same scene, one of them is going to look unnatural no matter which film you use. Here, the chefs' hats and the tops of their "whites" are lit by daylight, and appear as they should on daylight-balanced film. The rest of the scene is lit mainly by domestic tungsten and appears too orange on this type of film.

▷ **These pictures** illustrate the effects of mixing light sources and then photographing them with different types of film. This first shot was taken on ISO 160 tungsten light slide film not long before sunset, and you can see the unnatural coloration of the scene.

▷ **Taken within seconds** of the first picture, this version of the scene was recorded on ISO 64 daylight slide film. The image shows, essentially, the way colors would have looked if you had viewed the scene with your unaided eyes.

△ **Either daylight or tungsten film** could have been used for this image taken from a hotel balcony. The choice of a tungsten-balanced emulsion has brought up the blues and the reflections from the table settings catching the late sky light.

▷ **An hour later** the sun was down, and a 100-watt light bulb inside the tent was turned on. Recorded on the tungsten light film, you can see that the last traces of daylight in the sky appear very blue, but the tent, lit wholly by tungsten light, appears natural.

▷ **Taken within seconds** of the previous shot, but this time with the daylight-balanced film, the color of the sky has the rosy glow you associate with sunset pictures, but the tungsten-illuminated tent is far too orange to be considered natural.

△ **Tungsten film** has given a distinct blue cast to this isolated house, photographed at sunset. Balanced for the house lights, the film has produced purple tints that prevent the estuary setting looking prosaic.

◁ **Mismatched film and light sources** can give rise to interesting and colorful results. For this shot, daylight film was used and the distant multicolored neon and tungsten, some from passing cars, look very attractive. Exposure time was 2 seconds.

△ **The sumptuous interior** of the Ritz Hotel, London, has been captured using daylight film, and carefully balancing the daylight and tungsten lighting. Shooting on an overcast day ensured that the window illumination was not overpowering.

▽ **The rule** about matching film to the main light source has worked well here. Shot on daylight film, the snow has taken on a color cast from an early evening sky still rich in blue light, while the only artificial light, a tungsten bulb, looks invitingly warm.

Flash and daylight

Of all types of artificial light, electronic flash can most effectively be used to simulate daylight or to supplement it without altering its basic characteristics. Electronic flash is a form of easily portable daylight and can overcome a fundamental problem of photography in natural light – excessive contrast between highlights and shadows in the same scene. An exposure difference of two f stops between highlights and shadows is about the widest range film will handle comfortably (even less with slide film) – yet strong daylight falling into a room could indicate an exposure of f8 at $\frac{1}{500}$ second in a sunlit area, and only a step or two away in a shaded part of the room and exposure of f8 at $\frac{1}{30}$ second could be called for. This is a 16-fold fall-off in lighting intensity.

What is important to remember with flash is that its harshness can produce contrasty, over-sharp images unless it is used with judgment. The aim should be to reinforce the existing light to capture a scene rather than dramatically changing it by overlighting and killing the atmosphere. Using flash with daylight should enable the camera to match more closely the scene as seen with your eye by decreasing the contrast ratio while increasing the total amount of light.

△ **The studio flash unit** used for this photograph was aligned with the daylight entering from a window on the left of the camera position. This ensures that lighting direction is consistent, and conflicting shadows are thus avoided.

▷ **Built-in flash,** although not the most flexible of artificial light sources because of its fixed position, can nevertheless be extremely useful at times. To increase light levels generally inside this man's kitchen, the dedicated flash built into the camera perfectly regulated its output so as not to overwhelm the available daylight.

△ **The diamond anniversary** of this charming couple prompted me to duplicate the lighting in their original wedding photograph taken three decades earlier. To the weak daylight entering the studio, I added four flash tubes to the right of the camera position (in line with the daylight), and opposite the flashes I placed a large white reflector. This returned sufficient of the light spilling past them to fill the shadows and even out the contrast.

△ **The intense light** given off by the welding torch threw the rest of this sculptor's workshop into total darkness. To overcome this I chose a shutter speed of ⅛ second to record the sparks as trails of light, and then used fill-in electronic flash to illuminate the subject's face and show something of the background.

◁ **A common problem** when using daylight indoors is seen in this picture – excessive contrast. Exposure here was for the highlighted wall and the subject is underexposed.

◁ **The addition of electronic flash** has reduced the tonal range of the shot without killing the atmosphere of the daylight. The flash was heavily diffused to retain some shadow on the side of the subject away from the window.

▷ **Off-camera accessory flash** was used in this portrait of a shy young rider to brighten over-heavy shadows. After calculating the correct exposure settings for mixed daylight and flash, I draped two folds of a plain white handkerchief over the flash tube to soften its output.

Daylight, tungsten, and flash

A mixture of daylight and tungsten light is one of the most common forms of lighting encountered in indoor photography, especially in winter when daylight alone is usually too weak to light adequately the interior of even a small room. Light intensity can be increased by switching on room lights. These to our eyes will cast a neutral white light but on daylight film will appear very orange. For even more light, you can add electronic flash to the mixture. Because this type of light has about the same color temperature as daylight, it will enhance the daylight element of the scene. If you choose this type of lighting while using daylight-balanced film, then position the camera (or, if possible move the light sources) so that the orange glow of the tungsten enhances, rather than distracts attention from, the main subject.

If you use clear flash bulbs, however, then these are balanced for use with tungsten light film. With this type of film in the camera, it is the daylit elements of the scene that will display a color cast – this time a blue one.

△ **Electronic flash** aligned with daylight entering from windows was the principal light source for this portrait, but the overwarm color of the tungsten table lamp adds a welcome glow to the scene, which was shot on daylight-balanced film.

◁ **A combination** of existing room lights, candles, and clear flash bulbs bounced off a white ceiling have been combined to bring out the rich golds of the "priest's" vestments. I had to strike the right balance of illumination here in order to give the impression of the room being lit by candle light and also to show the background without distracting areas of deep shadow. The film used was balanced for use in tungsten light.

△ **The Malayan bridal couple** were photographed in a mixture of weak daylight reinforced by electronic flash and tungsten light from the chandelier and wall lights (out of shot). I positioned the flash midway between the camera and the subjects at a 45° angle and used daylight film. With this type of film, the tungsten light has given the room a strong green cast.

◁ **Accessory electronic flash** is immensely useful for candid reportage photography in situations such as the steamy interior of this Chinese restaurant in Hong Kong. The brief shutter speed used with the flash has made the street scene outside look much blacker than it was – enough daylight was coming in to affect exposure by about one-third of a stop. Although the picture was taken on daylight-balanced film, the orange glow of the bare tungsten bulb over the cook records that part of the room with all the authentic grittiness of the real thing.

▽ **The interior of this room** was lit principally by tungsten, and the daylight from the balcony was not sufficient to record the food in the foreground with completely natural colors on daylight film. To correct this, I used a small accessory flash directed just at the table, and a little extra illumination spilled past to relieve the dense shadow on the face and body of the waiter.

Unusual light sources

As both painters and photographers know, some of the most dramatic effects of light and shade are created by pictures in which the only source of illumination is a candle or some other form of dim light held by a figure half obscured by darkness. With today's fast lenses and sensitive emulsions, effective and evocative photographs can easily be taken with low-level artificial light sources, such as lamps, torches, or even the light from a single match, providing that you can overcome the problem of finding the best exposure balance.

The necessary slow shutter speeds needed for such low light levels always bring with them the danger of camera shake, so use a tripod or some other firm support. As in night photography, it is best to concentrate the restricted light source on the main point of interest in the picture and try to ensure that the area immediately surrounding it is no more than one f stop darker. This is normally possible only in the early evening, when the ebbing sun still provides enough ambient light to fill in a little detail in the shadowy areas surrounding the light source. The precise exposure will depend on the nearness of the light to the subject and the amount of light being reflected back.

△ **This dusk shot** of a factory shows how a combination of different colored lights can enliven a scene. Adding to fading daylight, mercury vapor lamps glow green and tungsten bulbs yellow.

▷ **The steelworker** in this scene is lit mainly by the rich gold and red glow of the furnace he has just tapped. Being rich in infrared radiation, the light gives a strong color cast entirely appropriate to the Dante-like scene.

◁ **Sodium vapor** street lighting is designed to help visibility in mist or fog, but has a distorting effect on the color of objects it illuminates. Due to the length of the exposure – 1½ seconds – areas of halation can be seen surrounding each lighting head.

▷ **A single match** was the only light source for this portrait, which says much about the versatility of modern lenses and films. Although tungsten-balanced film was used, the extremely low color temperature of the match flame has brought out warm tones in the girl's face.

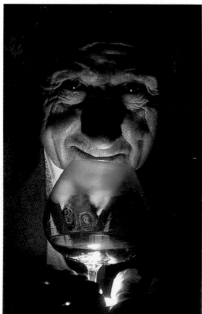

◁ **Low-angle lighting** has created a melodramatic, almost theatrical, look for this portrait. If the subject had had a less friendly face, however, the result could have looked sinister. The lighting effect was created by shining a narrow, high-intensity tungsten light up through the glass.

▷ **Mercury vapor lights** give a strong blue cast. Although the lips of the subject appear an odd hue, as does his vest, the colors throughout the scene are quite acceptable. Further interest is provided by orange tones of the tungsten lighting in the street behind him.

△ **Carefully positioned** and well-masked-down colored light sources were used to create this unusual portrait showing a model with a luminous green profile. Photographic colored gels were used over the fronts of the lights and the spread of the beams was controlled by cutting apertures in sheets of cardboard.

△ **Colored lights** are often used for theatrical effect to highlight areas of a scene. The picture of an egg in the palm of a hand was lit with a red spotlight in the ceiling and a blue light aimed at at the white screen that forms the background. The mixture of lights produces a white rim around the egg.

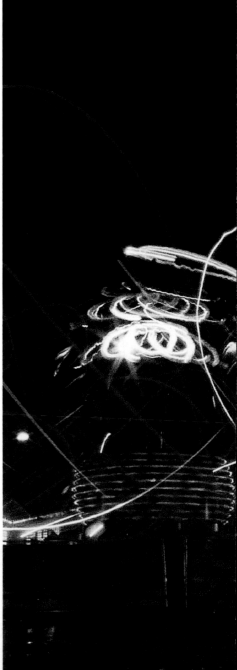

△ ▷ **Fairground lights** are intended to be bright and gaudy in order to attract as much attention as possible. No matter what type of film you use, color casts will be evident. For these two shots, daylight-balanced film was used. In the overall scene (above) the film has accurately recorded the inky blue of a cloudy dusk sky, and although the tungsten lights of the big wheel and red glow of the illuminated foreground roof look warmer than they really were, it really does not matter in this scene. To create the lighting effect in the large picture (right), a 2½-second exposure recorded a clear image of the stationery wheel and then, with the shutter still open, I took the camera off the tripod and waved it about for another few seconds.

◁ **Exploding fireworks** always look impressive seen against a completely black ground. The technique is a little hit and miss, since all you can do is point the camera in the right direction and hold the shutter open until you record two or three bursts.

Subject lighting

Portraits

Portraiture is one of the most enjoyable and rewarding areas of photography, and the simplest form of lighting is often the best. One lighting head can produce a wide range of effects. Used straight-on, however, it produces little form or modeling and flattens facial features. But when angled at 45°, both form and texture can be revealed. To reduce strong contrasts, using a reflector on the opposite side of the subject is often better than introducing another light, which can produce conflicting shadows. If a second light is used, it should be weaker than the first and used to accentuate specific parts of the subject – hands, for example, or the back of the head to give a slight rimlighting effect.

A successful portrait captures a person's essential character or style, which may be revealed in the face alone or indicated by pose, clothing, and setting. The subject should always feel at ease and you will have to learn to establish an instant rapport with all manner of people. The setting should always support the subject. An ideal lens to use is one that allows you to fill the frame with the subject without approaching too closely. For the 35mm format, a lens in the range 90–120mm is a popular choice – 150mm for medium-format cameras.

◁**In this simply lit photograph,** the artist Carel Weight poses with a painting of the author Roald Dahl, his latest commission. The studio setting for the picture had ample indirect daylight, ideal for both painting and photography, and all that had to be added was a white reflector to even out the contrast on the shadowy side of the subject.

◁**A judiciously cleaned mirror** shows just enough of the subject's far profile to balance the composition perfectly. By using a medium long lens (135mm on a 35mm camera) I was able to fill the frame while using the limited depth of field inherent with this type of lens to knock the reflected image just slightly out of focus. If the reflection had been equally sharp, the dual points of interest would have weakened the atmosphere and mood of the picture.

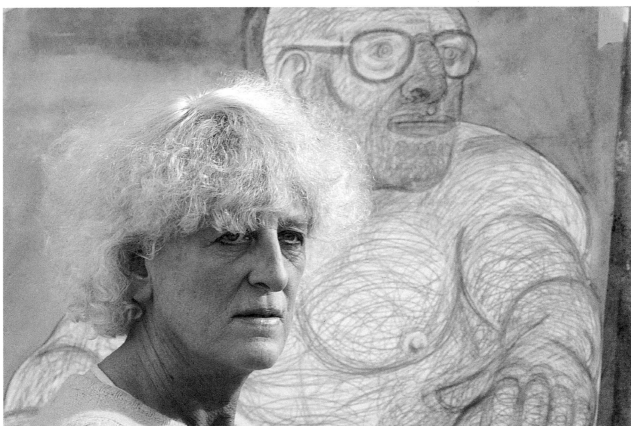

◁**This powerful image** shows the reflection of the sitter in his bedroom mirror with a framed portrait of his son on the dressing table in front. Lighting for the sitter was simple window light, but in order to balance the illumination the framed picture was lit with slightly diffused flash.

◁**The simplicity and color** of Cecil Beaton's clothes contrast strongly with the elaborate bust he is leaning against. Beaton's expression is enquiring, his pose nonchalant, suggesting the relaxed attitude of a man more at ease with other photographers and their equipment than most. Bright light from a window provided the only form of lighting.

△ **Photographed in her own studio,** the artist Elizabeth Frink looks perfectly relaxed. The artist's hair coloring, clothing, and the light-toned image behind have all worked perfectly together to produce a classic portrait. Natural daylight was the only illumination and the lens used was an 80–210mm zoom set at 90mm.

△ **Fading light** at evening on a beach in Indonesia provided a sympathetic atmosphere for this portrait of an old fisherwoman, who is crowned by a piece of coral and the turquoise bowl she has been using to collect seafood and shells. Despite her bare feet and ragged clothes, she maintains an overwhelming sense of dignity.

△ **Shooting from a squatting position** helps to emphasize the height of this Senegalese horseman and draw attention to the ancient rifle he is proudly holding. However, the most surprising aspect of this portrait is the subject's startling crown of brilliant red, which helps to differentiate him from the background of sky.

◁ **Bold and uncompromising framing** is often the best approach to this type of portraiture. The subject, brought up large in the frame by a 135mm telephoto lens, is tonally very similar to the background. But the limited depth of field produced by an aperture of f4.5 has thrown everything but the subject completely out of focus.

◁ **Framed by her own hair,** the model's face was too much in shadow for a successful portrait. To overcome this, I placed a small bronze-colored reflector on the floor in front of her, angled upward so that a little extra daylight was bounced up and into her face.

▽ **Spotlit by a beam of sunlight,** the model seems transfixed. In situations like this, take care not to let the highlight influence your exposure reading, unless you want a more mysterious-looking image with most of the subject's face underexposed.

◁ ▽ **Not until your film is developed** is it possible to tell if a portrait session has really been a success. An afternoon photo session with the novelist and playwright JB Priestley had been extremely enjoyable, his natural graciousness, wit, and good humor making the time fly by. His choice of clothing had been his own, and to overcome the heavy shadows – cast by the brim of his hat – obscuring his eyes, I used weak, reflected flash from almost floor level. At my direction, I photographed him with and without his pipe, but the shot with his briar firmly clamped in his teeth is by far the most characteristic and successful image of the session. Without the pipe, his face somehow looks unfinished.

△ **When communication is a problem** because you don't speak the same language as your subjects, the results can sometimes look a little awkward. If the rooster being held by the woman was not such a peculiar addition to the scene, these two may have seemed too unrelaxed and wooden.

▷ **Double portraits often benefit** from the subjects being on distinctly different levels – but the trick is to bring this situation about in an entirely natural fashion. Here, I used the raised verandah as the ideal device to lift the woman up above the level of her husband, who was posed on the ground below.

▷ **A formal solution** for a formal group portrait. With this number of people to encompass in the one shot, you will need to string them out in a single line if you are to avoid heads and bodies getting in the way of other members of the group, unless you rank them with some standing behind others who are sitting. When your subjects are wearing broad-rimmed hats such as these, be careful that their faces don't become lost in shadow. If tilting their heads slightly back looks unnatural, use a reflector low down in front of them to bounce some light up into their faces, or use heavily diffused flash.

◁ **This informal group** at a refreshment stall in Kuala Lumpur was photographed with a long lens in diffused sunlight. The pale pinks, yellows, and browns, the relaxed pose of the man lighting his pipe, and the slight movement on the figure of the child who had just slipped off her father's knee all contribute to the peaceful atmosphere of the composition.

◁ **The middle figure** engages the viewer by looking directly into the camera lens, while her two friends, one in the foreground and the other in the background, look studiously in opposite directions. The colors and textures of their sweaters act like stepping stones, taking you back, stage by stage, into the frame.

▷ **Candid group shots,** such as this one of an informal jazz trio on board a cruise boat, are usually best undertaken using at least a moderately long lens (here 90mm on a 35mm camera). With a lens like this, you can hang back from the action, where the presence of the camera will not interfere, and still bring the subjects up good and large in the frame.

Nudes

Photographs that isolate facets of a nude figure through lighting, cropping, or angle of view can create striking abstract patterns, especially when shooting in black and white. Color, however, lends itself to a less depersonalized approach to photographing the human form. Indirect daylight can reveal all the subtleties of shape and form through tonal gradations, while stronger, more directional light and harsher subject contrast will create a bolder mood – if that is your intention.

Background, viewpoint, and lighting should all be related to the characters of the models and the qualities they convey – innocent or sensual, for example, or romantic or erotic. Dim, secretive lighting can be effective if the model feels vulnerable, or is able to convey that impression in front of the camera, while a provocatively confident model, male of female, may respond to more revealing lighting that produces stronger contrasts.

When working with a new model, you need to study your subject to see how his or her body can best be modeled with light and shadow, and remember that in avoiding blatancy, the expression is often more important than the pose.

◁ **A graceful candor** can be captured at moments when a model is offguard and un-selfconscious. During a break in shooting, and thus not concentrating on the camera, the model raised her arms to stretch as window light spread all around her body. The simplicity and beauty of her stance is helped by a neutral expression.

◁ **A poignant vulner-ability** is conveyed as this woman clasps her arms across her breasts. To give the soft lighting, electronic flash was diffused and masked so that its illumination fell just in front of her body. I took the picture through a sheet of glass, using the steam from a kettle for the condensation.

▷ **Patterns of sunlight** rake the body of a woman who seems almost a victim of the warmth in which she basks. The pose is unconventional, light flattening her breasts. But the picture is an intriguing composition in yellows and browns, light and shade, hardness and softness.

◁ **A combination of water** and nakedness can produce a mood of delicate eroticism. The girl floating in the pool was lit by harsh and powerful sunlight that gives the picture great luminosity and depth. The disturbed surface of the water conceals as much as it reveals.

▷ **A different approach to lighting** often suits the male nude. Generally, diffused light tends to be best for a woman's body, but for a man experiment with more undiffused side-lighting, and keep fill-in light to a minimum. This type of lighting accentuates the muscle groups and emphasizes the subject's masculinity.

Children

Spontaneity is the essence of successfully photographing children. It is for this reason that many photographers prefer to take pictures of children out of doors, where they can move around freely, or informally in their own homes, rather than in the strange and unfamiliar surroundings of a studio.

Gentle directional sunlight is ideal, both because it allows you to work from any angle, with or against the light, and because its soft, even quality brings out the fresh color and smooth texture of young complexions.

The volatility of a child's moods means that quick reflexes and a degree of pre-planning are needed to capture a characteristic gesture or expression. For candid shots outdoors, you may find it useful to work out exposures on the basis of shooting with a shutter speed of ½₅₀ second, or at least ½₁₂₅ second, but no slower. If you stick with these sorts of shutter speeds you will be able to take rapid shots at various angles and directions, changing the shooting position as necessary, while minimizing the chance of pictures being spoiled by camera movement. And if you are using a long lens to keep a reasonable distance between yourself and your subject, a fast shutter speed becomes even more important.

△ **A wallowing buffalo,** two grinning children, and low evening light, which brings out the rich greens in the field behind them, make up a composition that balances subdued tones and bright highlights.

▽ **Candid shots** such as this rather forlorn looking boy, have to be taken as found. I would rather have reoriented him slightly but any interference on my part would have changed the character and nature of the picture.

◁ **When photographing children in the studio** it is sensible to have plenty of activities your subjects can throw themselves into. For this picture, I used two studio flashes, both fitted with softboxes to give a broad, flexible lighting scheme, and waited until the little girl was totally absorbed in her painting before starting to shoot. I don't think she even knew I had taken her picture.

▽ **The diffused evening light** in which I took this shot of a confident young boy and his shy sister was strong enough to produce highlights on their hair but soft enough to shows colors as fully saturated. Although the terraced paddy-field makes a complicated background, it is shadowy and subdued, and links up with the striped pattern of the boy's tee-shirt.

◁ **Ready for bed** on a still-bright summer's evening, this young girl was happy to pose for the camera along as she could cuddle her favorite teddy-bear. The only addition to the light entering through the bedroom window is a small reflector propped up against the tripod and angled upward toward her face.

▽ **Bright daylight and slight overexposure** have subdued the strong carnival colors of the costumes of these Spanish children, allowing attention to be focused on their individual facial expressions – serious, detached, and impish.

△ **A wide-angle lens,** here a 28mm lens used on a 35mm camera, used close up and from above noticeably distorts perspective, as you can see in this portrait. The little girl's forehead appears overly large and her head too big for her body. This type of effect can be used occasionally as a special effect.

▷ **Center-weight metering,** if the subject is large in the frame and centrally positioned, is fine to use in snow scenes, as exposure will be biased in favor of the subject and less so for the surrounding whiteness.

△ **Dappled sunshine** was the light source for this double portrait of identically dressed brothers. Their close relationship is obvious to all, but it is especially evident in the protective arm the older boy has placed around his young brother's shoulders.

◁ **Close relationships** are also shown in this portrait, accentuated by the unselfconscious pose of the children. Exposure here was for the highlights, but contrast was not so great that their faces were lost in shadow.

▽ **Photographed in a dark Bombay alleyway** you can see just how well the children's olive skins harmonize with the background colors. The low camera angle helps to separate the subjects from their visually complex surroundings, and by using a moderate telephoto lens I could keep back and not run the risk of them playing to the camera.

◁ **Care needs to be taken** when you are photographing in color that your working light is not tainted by unwanted color casts from nearby surfaces. In this Moroccan interior, the room was lined with the mellow shades of carved wooden panels, which imparted an attractive rosiness to the daylight from large windows to the left of the camera position.

Still life

Still-life pictures are studied arrangements of inanimate objects that give the photographer the luxury of time and complete control. Such pictures may be assembled with patient care, or chanced upon. From a photographic point of view, if you were to study any found arrangement of ornaments in your own home you would probably have the makings of a still-life composition.

In making still lifes, you can give full rein to your imagination, selecting objects that are constantly used but rarely seen as shapes, forms, and textures of intrinsic aesthetic interest. To give coherence to the picture it is necessary to have a clear idea of its central theme. Lighting is of crucial importance. For identification, soft, shadowless, diffused light is often most effective, and you can use reflectors to suggest form without introducing harsh shadows. If more contrast is needed, directional lighting will dramatize form and texture, and a selective light source, such as a spotlight, allows you precise control of shadows and highlights.

When building an arrangement it is best to view it constantly through the camera in the approximate lighting you will be using. A tripod is a good idea, and the effect should be of only one light source, even if more are used.

△ ▷ **Everyday objects** can make effective subjects for a still-life composition. In these examples, I used the attractive shape an old-fashioned wire egg basket sitting on the stone-topped work surface of my kitchen. For the the first shot (above), I simply took one egg out and placed it on the side, along with some feathers. For the next version (right), I added an old milk jug for balance. Lighting for both pictures was window light.

△ **Moving in closer** by using a longer lens, the framing is now much tighter and the heavily textured back wall is no longer in view. The egg basket on the right of the frame looked unbalanced until I added the wicker basket. The framed picture of roosters and chickens was an amusingly appropriate addition. A white reflector was needed to balance the daylight.

◁ **Carrying on the theme of yesteryear,** this composition shows the same egg basket but now propped with an old bread barrel, clock, and candle holder. Although the principal light source is still window light, the burning candle has a much lower color temperature and throws a suitably mellow cast over the scene.

◁ **High contrast**
between the china egg
cup and saucer and the
slab of black polished
stone they rest on give
these two images
greater dramatic impact
than the more rustic
theme of the other still
lifes on these pages. I
judged the first image
(above left) to be a little
too stark in its simplicity,
so for the second
version (below left) I
carefully sliced the top
off the egg and
arranged it on one side
of the saucer, with two
small fragments of
broken shell on the
other side to give the
composition a greater
sense of balance. For
both pictures, I used
reflected studio flash
from a white-colored
flash umbrella set up
on the left of the egg.
On the opposite side I
balanced a small square
of white cardboard to
return the light spilling
past and prevent
shadows becoming
too dense.

▷ **Changing to a**
macro lens has
completely altered the
mood of this still-life
subject. Rather than
being an arrangement
of eggs, the emphasis
has now shifted to the
repeating shapes of
their rounded outlines,
bisected by the bars
of the wire basket, and
their softly textured
shells. The warm color
cast is the result of
using the candle (seen
opposite) close in to
the subject.

△ **This collection of Victoriana** is so arranged that no one piece dominates. Light was diffused by greaseproof paper over a window on one side and a white cardboard reflector on the other. I shot directly down on the arrangement, which was laid out on the floor, and because window light alone was used, exposure time was 1 second.

▷ **Neatly ordered ranks** allow you to see and appreciate individual pieces in this collection of collectible toys, film cartons, and other domestic items. In style, both content and composition, it could not be more different to the casual arrangement in the still life above. Lighting was direct flash either side of the camera position.

▷ **A simple subject,** yet the reflective qualities of glass always need careful handling. Lit from behind by window light, I used a flash umbrella on the far side, but only as a reflector (no flash was attached to it) to help balance contrast and better define the form of the decanter and water glasses.

◁ **Colors, textures, shapes, and forms** abound in this collection of fruits of the sea. The commercial demand for food photography from magazines and book publishers, super-markets and advertisers is insatiable. Here, the fish, crabs, oysters, and prawns all look temptingly fresh and appetising and the propping, which is simple and attractive, acts to promote the product rather than overwhelm it.

◁ **Found still lifes** abound, both in nature and about the home. This dusty collection of left-over bits and pieces, which had been placed on an attic shelf over a period of decades, required no re-arrangement at all, and I shot it just as I found it using window light to backlight the subjects.

▷ **A worn leather boot** grained wood, bark and stripped wood, and a knotted rope end provide color harmonies and contrasting textures that clearly define the forms. A low, directional spotlight was the main light source, and the whole arrangement was encircled with white reflectors.

Architecture and detailing

To bring architectural subjects to life, lighting is of paramount importance, since it can dramatize a derelict building or make the most adventurous structure look dull and uninteresting. The response to light of each building material thus needs to be appreciated – the reflections in glass at different angles, for example. Concrete structures tend to show up well in full sunshine with solid shadows; stone relief work needs more delicate, directional lighting to reveal form; and iron or steel structures make striking abstract patterns when backlit. Strong sidelighting, highlighting some surfaces and throwing others into shadow, provides modeling and texture, while diffused light may be better when you want to show subtleties of color. Buildings located on high ground, such as cathedrals, can frequently be shot from a distance with a long lens. A shift lens, or a camera with a rising back and front, is essential for photographing without distortion buildings of any height, as is a sturdy tripod. The inclusion of a figure can emphasize a point of interest as well as give a sense of scale, but it is best to avoid brightly clad crowds. And bear in mind that even if it is not possible to shoot an entire building there may be areas of architectural detailing worthy of your attention.

▷ **The majestic colonnade** of St Peter's Basilica in the Vatican City is given a sense of scale by the inclusion of a single, dark-clad figure. His off-center positioning in no way prevents the eye looking deep into the frame.

◁ **Look for imaginative** ways to frame a building when you cannot move far enough back to include it all. By adopting a camera position at the very base of one of the the structures and then angling the camera slightly, the buildings form a strong, diagonal line that gives vitality to the composition.

▷ **Finding high ground** to shoot from was the best way of recording this complex of buildings making up an extensive country home while showing something of its parkland setting.

◁ **Stongly converging vertical lines** result from pointing a lens, especially a wide-angle, up to include the top of a tall building. This effect become apparent when the the film plane is not parallel with the subject. This picture gains added impact by shooting through the transparent top of a pedestrian tunnel at the base of the building.

◁ **A glass façade** glimmers with light and color that add depth to a piece of striking modern architecture. To avoid the effect of a black wall, which a shot in full sun would have produced, I waited for the softer light of sunset to be reflected in the glass with neon lights shining below.

▷ **It is color** that lifts these utilitarian farm buildings out of the ordinary. Bathed in the warmth of afternoon sunlight, they seems to glow in contrast to the shadowy foreground, yet seem well separated form the foliage and cliff face behind.

◁ **The intriguingly irregular** walls, windows, and supporting oak beams of this ancient Tudor building create an interesting abstract design when seen within the well-defined edges of the picture frame. Apart from the purple-colored door, this shot could almost have been taken on black and white film.

◁ **Unusual camera positions** will be necessary to record some architectural features. To take this magnificent vaulted ceiling in a Gothic cathedral, I had to lie flat on my back, resting the camera against my face for the ⅛-second exposure that was needed in the dim light coming from the high windows.

▷ **The hard edges of the viewfinder** frame have been used to good advantage here to isolate the geometric form and saturated color of a segment of a clapboard building. Slightly overcast lighting ensured a near shadowless result.

▽ **Buildings do not have to be old or beautiful** to make worthy subjects for the camera. Even if a building has no particular architectural merit, choosing the right viewpoint and shooting at the time of day when the light is most effective can make all the difference. Here, the regular repetitive shapes of these warehouse windows is what drew my attention, and I was careful to make sure that the segment of the façade I selected included the one open shutter in that entire wall.

Animals and wildlife

To succeed as an animal photographer you need to be a bit of a naturalist as well, because half the skill is understanding the behavior of your subjects. However, quick reflexes, alertness, familiarity with your equipment, and patience are all required in large measure, too. You may need to spend long hours in a hide or under natural cover waiting for the right moment to shoot, and if luck is not on your side the wait may be fruitless or the picture results disappointing.

Light conditions for animal and wildlife photography can be extremely difficult. Many wild animals appear in the open only in poor light. Long exposures are rarely possible, since animals move quickly and often in unpredictable ways, forcing you into a reliance on fast film, fast telephoto lenses, silent shutters, and quiet film-advance motors. Accurate TTL (through-the-lens) exposure meters and quick autofocus lenses help to give you an edge.

If your animal subject is an elusive, wild creature or a domestic pet, try to portray it in a sympathetic setting. If a background is intrusive, use depth of field to knock it out of focus or, with a moving subject, pan the camera using a slowish shutter speed to reduce the surroundings to an abstract blur.

⊲ **A local bird sanctuary** was the setting for this animal study. Fully recovered after injuring itself, and nearly ready for release back into the wild, this owl would have been impossible to find in the open like this during daylight hours.

▷ **A wide lens aperture** on a 300mm telephoto has produced such a limited depth of field in this shot that the background, which would have been very confusing, has blurred beyond recognition. This provides the contrast needed to give the monkeys a sharp outline.

⊲ **Diffused frontal lighting,** in combination with toplighting coming from the rear of this young chick, has suppressed some of the detail in its still spiky feathers, but it has created a powerful image in which shape is the predominant subject feature.

▷ **The quality of an animal's fur,** such as that of these pedigree cats, is best depicted using undiffused light. Here, I used a single studio flash head to the right of the camera position and reflector boards on the other side of the animals in order to prevent contrast becoming a factor.

▷ **Natural-looking enclosures** found in modern zoos make pictures such as this shot of a rare white tiger look as if they were taken in the wild. The extensive depth of field is the clue here – if the picture had been taken with an extreme telephoto, as would be necessary in the wild, the background would not be nearly so sharp. The photograph was, in fact taken with a zoom lens set at 210mm.

△ **A quite, steady approach** was necessary to approach this crocodile without scaring it back into the water or perhaps provoking an attack. The reptile knew I was there but I made sure there was always a healthy distance between us.

▷ **Chimpanzees soon become semi-tame** if they are in constant contact with people. This youngster lived in a troop on a regular tourist route and had become accustomed to accepting offerings of food from the visitors. Showing no apprehension at all, it seemed perfectly happy to pose for the camera.

▽ **Taken from this angle** it is impossible to tell that this is not a picture of a wild fox. It is, in fact, a domesticated animal, having been taken in as an orphaned cub. A high camera viewpoint is not always appropriate for small subjects, but it can help to eliminate a cluttered or intrusive background.

△ **The limited angle of view** of a telephoto lens is the perfect cropping device if used with insight. By shooting with a 250mm lens (on a 35mm camera) it was possible to eliminate all aspects of the surroundings and show nothing but the parrots.

△ **Frogs will often freeze** when they think they are in danger, working on the principle that if they don't move they cannot be seen. This allowed me to approach within a few feet of this small frog and use a short telephoto lens wide open at f2.8.

▷ **Composition is paramount,** even when the subject is as photogenic as this black swan. Moving the camera so that the swan was at the side of the frame brought the duck into view and helped to balance the composition. The background, although soft, adds vital extra information to the picture.

Sporting activities

Lighting levels for indoor sporting activities are seldom adequate to record fast-moving events, and electronic flash must nearly always be used to support the floodlights or spotlights normally present in the arena. Accessory flash used on the camera tends to give a rather flat image without much form. It is best to set up your flash units at an angle to the subject, using a flash synchronization cable and slave units to make sure they fire at precisely the right instant. The limited range of this flash in large, open areas can work to your advantage by underexposing the background – thus hiding any tangle of ropes, bars, and wires that may be present. Fast film and lenses are usually needed, but anticipation of the right moment to trip the shutter is really crucial

Outdoor sport can be played under conditions ranging from dazzling sunlight to near darkness. Strong light makes it easier to capture the energy of an event because you will have the chance to select very brief shutter speeds to stop the action dead. Apart from fast lenses and film, the basic technical requirement for outdoor work is a versatile camera with interchangeable lenses, or a fixed-lens camera with a zoom covering a wide range of focal lengths.

△ **Timing is vital** when photographing this type of sporting activity. A second before or after and the swimmer's face, turned to the side to suck in a quick breath, and arm would not have been in the correct position for this dynamic image.

▽ **The excitement** of this image has been enhanced by the camera position – low down at the very base of the fence looking up at the horse and rider. Using a wide-angle lens has distorted the foreground perspective, adding drama to the picture.

▽ **A strong spotlight** behind the gymnast was used to create the atmosphere of this picture. This, however, did not produce sufficient illumination and so a subsidiary flash unit was aligned with the spotlight and another was set up to the left of the camera position.

◁ **Natural daylight** was used to take this shot of sumo wrestlers competing as part of a training session. Flash would have killed the atmosphere of the scene so I deliberately set a shutter speed (⅛ second) that would record slight subject blur. This best expressed the way I experienced the event.

▷ **Taken in thickening fog** this picture of a rugby tackle has a grimy quality that helps to evoke the mud and toil of the game. Locked together in equal exhaustion at the end of the match, the players could be seen clearly only from a distance of about 30 ft (9 m).

△ **The bright conditions** on a snow field in full sunshine give you the flexibility to select a really fast shutter speed in order to "freeze" subject movement. A slightly blurred or panned image would express the movement of the snowboarder, but then you would miss seeing the large lumps of snow and dust thrown up into the air.

◁ **A general light reading** taken from this scene could cause exposure problems. The amount of light reflecting back from the undisturbed snow is far brighter than the light reflecting back from the subject, and so underexposure of the skier could result. If your camera allows, in situations such as this use center-weighted metering or, better still, spot metering. If this is not possible, take a light reading from the back of your hand in sunshine and lock that setting into the camera.

▷ **Sporting action pictures** place a requirement on the photographer to be fit and, often, to know something of the sport being photographed. Even when all proper precautions have been taken, rock climbing still retains an element of danger. Timing was crucial in this shot, for as soon as the descending climber moved out of the shadow I had set exposure for, she would have been lost against the overexposed tree tops far below.

△ **A good selection of lens focal lengths** is a prerequisite for much sports photography, since you never know when the action is going to explode virtually at your feet, when a wide-angle may be your best choice, or in the far distance, when you will need a powerful telephoto lens. For this picture of a hang-glider I used a 200mm lens (on a 35mm camera) and a x2 teleconverter to double its effective focal length.

◁ **Age is no barrier** to physical fitness, as this picture of an elderly singles oarsman demonstrates. The setting, a quiet stretch of river on a sunless winter's day, is not particularly exciting, but the undeniable power of the photograph comes from the use of a wide-angle lens close to the prow of the subject's boat. To take the picture I lay out flat, over the back of the leading motor boat, with the camera just inches above the water.

◁ ▽ **White water canoeing** is fast, exciting, colorful, and can be dangerous. The speed of the participants as they flash past your camera position can be the most difficult aspect of covering this activity. But the more you study the action the more opportunities you should see. Once you have found a good shooting position, on the bank or an overhead bridge, you will notice that the canoes all tend to take a similar route through the rapids. This allows you to prefocus and set exposure for a specific part of the watery course, and then wait for the action to enter the viewfinder.

Underwater photography

Taking photographs underwater can be a startling experience, especially for a newcomer to diving. Apart from the cathedral-like silence, the vividness of colors and abundance of life in warmer, clearer waters are a revelation. The chief problem of underwater photography is the reduced light levels. Even in the clearest water, seven-eighths of daylight is lost at at depth of only 35 ft (11 m). As well, the minute particles suspended in the water – plankton, minerals, sand, and so on – tend to scatter what light does penetrate. Because of this, it is best to restrict yourself to the top 20 ft (6 m) of water and to use fast – ISO 1600–3200 – film. Even so, you may still have to supplement the available light with electronic flash, and as a rough guide to exposure, divide the surface flash factor by four. If photographed head-on, body shape and the sometimes iridescent colors of marine fish are not at all obvious. For this reason, try to record them from an angle. Don't forget the need for an interesting background for your subjects – rocks, weed, or sand are all preferable to seeing fish in open water, which will probably record as featureless black and make the subject take on a rather two-dimensional appearance.

△ **The remarkable camouflage** of this prickly leatherjacket, which looks almost like a cave painting, from the waters of Southeast Asia attracted my attention in an aquarium. To avoid reflections from the glass, I lit the tank by flash from above.

▷ **This sea anemone,** exposing its turquoise interior and wonderful markings, was shot through a glass-bottomed box in shallow water on Australia's Great Barrier Reef. Although you are more limited in terms of the subject matter you will encounter when working in this way, you do not have to invest in any specialized water-proof equipment.

△ **Marine life** found in tidal pools or on coastal reefs can often be photographed with an ordinary camera. This example of dead coral, with its shapely, radiating spines, had just been uncovered by the retreating tide on the Great Barrier Reef of Australia.

◁ **The brilliant coloring** of this regal tang illustrates the advantage of photographing fish against a background that provides interest, scale, and contrast. I selected a slow shutter speed to record a faint image of the rocks and other fish, and the slight traces of subject movement prevent the subject looking static.

Materials and techniques

Selecting the exposure

Gauging the correct exposure for color film is much more critical than for black and white, yet it is usually possible to vary the exposure by about one stop on either side and still produce acceptable results. Printing allows you further latitude for correction by at least a stop or two either way without much loss of color fidelity or detail. Modern TTL (through-the-lens) exposure meters are accurate enough to keep you within these limits in wide-ranging lighting conditions. Many cameras now allow you to switch metering modes from center-weighted to averaging and, sometimes, to spot metering as well.

Problems generally arise when you are shooting against the light, in extreme conditions, or if there are areas of strong tonal contrast. In these situations you have to decide what balance to strike between bright highlights and deep shadow areas. The alternative is to shoot only in flat, even lighting, and results will then often lack drama or impact.

Underexposure by up to half a stop generally produces saturated color in reversal films, and overexposure by a similar amount has similar results with color negatives. Since the mood of a color picture can be radically changed by such adjustments, exposure must be carefully considered. Landscapes will appear richer by underexposing half a stop or more, for example, whereas portraits of women are often more effective with a slight degree of overexposure.

△ **The pattern of light and shade** in this portrait was captured by exposing for detail and richness in the highlights. This resulted in the dense, encroaching shadows suggesting the secrecy of a forest. The bulk and form of the tree trunk is accentuated by the angular light. An averaging light reading for this scene was f8, but the actual exposure used was f11 (both at ½₅ second).

▽ **The sequence** shown here demonstrates the effect that exposure has on form, atmosphere, and color. A range of apertures was used in daylight using ISO 100 film and a shutter speed of ¹⁄₆₀ second.

△ **f2** This degree of overexposure weakens color and substance.

△ **f2.8** Less than a stop's difference and no substantial improvement.

△ **f4** Color now is better and this would make a suitable high-key shot.

△ **f5.6** Color is bright and well-defined and this is probably the best exposure.

△ **f8** This exposure also gives perfectly acceptable results.

△ **f11** Color saturation is now more apparent, ideal for low-key shots.

△ **f16** This level of underexposure and shadow detail is beginning to go.

△ **f22** Colors are now very muddy, degraded, and heavy looking.

◁ **Although about a stop** under-exposed, the ornate exterior of this cathedral would have lost much of its power and presence and richness of tone if it had been recorded at the recommended settings.

▷ **The man whittled away** by the distant, intense sunlight seems insubstantial against the massively underexposed interior of the corridor. Over- and underexposure produce a powerfully graphic and abstract image.

▽ **Fan vaulting** in the ceiling of Wells Cathedral was difficult to photograph because of the intense light from the high windows. Rather than make any exposure allowance for these highlights, I decided to give 1½ stops extra exposure on a reading taken from the shadows. This high-key approach has emphasized the delicate tracery of the column tops and roof struts.

Camera manipulation

Effective manipulated images seldom emerge by accident – they most often require careful thought and advance preparation if they are to be truly effective. Almost any combination of images can be tried, since it is quite easy to select certain areas and mask out others. Most often, however, simple images combined with patterned ones have the greatest impact. Imagination and perception are more important than complicated camera techniques or lighting set-ups. Apart from being fun, experiments with mixed or altered images provide a visual jolt that can compel us to reassess familiar objects. When seen on a different scale and in a different setting, everyday things can take on an entirely new significance.

One easy way to use the camera to manipulate the familiar world around us is by double exposure – that is, taking two, or more, pictures on the same frame of film. However, most cameras today have automatic film advance and so do not allow you to try this. Instead, experiment with "sandwiching" processed slides, or slides and negatives, in the same mount, projecting them together, and photographing the result. Slightly thin negatives and slides give best results.

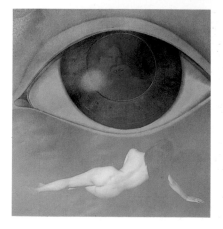

◁ ▷ **Double exposure in the camera** has produced these two results. The huge changes of scale in the first image (left) was produced by photographing the eye from a magazine using a macro lens. The position of the bottom of the eye was noted and then the photograph of the model was shot on the same frame of film against a black velvet background using a standard lens. The same technique was used for the next image (right), and the simple background allows the face to show clearly. All components were underexposed by about a stop.

◁ **Simple mixed media** techniques have been employed to give us this striking image. Different photographs were the sources for the cut-out eyes and startling red mouth. These were stuck onto flexible black plastic, lit, and photographed. The smearing of the light results from slightly flexing and twisting the plastic base.

◁ **Lens attachments,** such as the prism attachment used for this image, are a straight-forward way of manipulating familiar subjects. Used normally, a prism filter will split the image, vertically or horizontally, to produce overlapping or wholly separate subjects. Here, however, the prism attachment was turned during the 2-second night-time exposure.

▷ **This could be** the type of picture you might expect from a badly tuned TV set. Using different-colored filters for each exposure, a normal image was recorded on slide film. A selection of these false-color slides were then projected together, slightly offset, to give the overlapping colors. As soon as you see an effect you like, take a record of it on slide film for projection or negative film for prints.

◁ ▷ **Projecting patterns** onto the human form can produce effects ranging from subtle and intriguing alterations to powerful and surreal distortions. In the first shot (left), a carefully aligned image of a heavily textured surface gives the face of the model a mask-like appearance that could be an illustration for a science-fiction subject. In the next shot (right) the black and white lines of the projected image wrap around the model, molding themselves to every undulation of her body.

Computer manipulation

The advent of fast and inexpensive computer-processing chips and the ready availability of image-scanners have opened up a complete new world of near-instantaneous, highly controllable, and endlessly repeatable image manipulations. However, due to the heavy demand these techniques make on computer memory, you still require, apart from the appropriate software, a reasonably powerful desktop computer.

To a large extent, computers have done away with many of the old darkroom craft skills, such a burning and dodging (used to manipulate local print density in black and white printing), as well as a whole range of color techniques, including retouching, solarization, posterization, air-brush effects, toning, coloring, and multiple printing (in which parts of two or more negatives or slides are printed on one piece of paper to make a single, composite image).

But computer manipulations are not used just to create radical changes in an original film image, all manner of corrective techniques are also available, including sharpening or blurring, removing or minimizing the appearance of film grain, and the removal or addition of subject elements to help composition.

△ **This still-life grouping** of clay jugs is a straight print from the original film image. The slide was scanned into the computer using a high-resolution setting. If you use a digital camera to record the original image, scanning is then not needed.

◁ **1 The first stage** in this exercise was to "cut out" electronically the small jug on the right of the group, deleting not only the other jugs but also the table on which they stood. The original background was also deleted and new blue-gray one "pasted in", graduated in tone to mimic the sidelighting used on the subject.

▷ **2 A new table top** has now been added. You can insert any of a wide variety of backgrounds held in digital form. Many examples are included as part of the software, or you could shoot one or more specifically to suit an idea you have and then scan them into the computer. In this example, a mahogany effect has been used.

◁ **3 To heighten the realism** of this newly created image, a shadow has been electronically painted on to the surface of the table top. To do this, all you need do is specify the area of the table you want to appear darker than the rest. Take note of the angle of the lighting when deciding where to place shadows.

▷ **4 Once it is electronically decorated** the jug takes on a completely new appearance, one that would pass as being utterly authentic. The stripes and other motifs were added using a retouching tool (which is shaped like a paintbrush) so that the textures and tones of the original jug show through the color.

△ △ **The original image** can be seen above. The idea was to show the decorated Moroccan plate against a sympathetic background, but on reflection it was decided that the background was simply too overpowering. To salvage the picture, the original slide was scanned into the computer and the tiled background replaced by a neutral-toned one. To stop the bowl looking like it was floating above its new setting, a radial graduated tint was applied to the background – creating shadows in the corners of the frame. Finally, to anchor the bowl firmly, a shadow was placed underneath it corresponding to the one you can see in the original picture.

△ ▷ **Digital retouching** can be used to bring about seamless changes to your pictures. In the original shot (above) a high-altitude vapor trail from a jet creates a distracting white line at the top of the frame, and there is also a slight scratch to the right of the powdery snow above the board. On the retouched version (right) both these faults were removed by copying nearby tones and pasting them into the problem areas. As a final touch, the yellow of the subject's jacket was also strengthened.

△ ▷ **Colors not known in nature** do not represent a problem to the electronic palette. The real colors of the hibiscus flower can be seen above. In the manipulated version (right), the colors of the pollen and the petals have been swapped to produce a bizarre-looking new variety. To bring about changes like this, all you need to do is highlight the specific areas of the picture on the screen and then choose a new color from the range presented by the software. Standard reference numbers can also be entered to bring about color changes.

△ **Prints as well as transparencies** can be scanned. The original image used here was a black and white print, and all of the false color could have been created traditionally, using bleaching and hand-coloring techniques. But computer manipulation allows you to alter colors virtually at will, and you need stop only when you see a combination you like.

◁ **This apparent mirror-image picture** is the result of combining parts of two different originals. The first is of the girl, who was photographed in the studio against a neutral-toned background. After the picture was scanned, the girl was cut away from the background and a copy image flipped to give a laterally reversed version, which was then combined with the original. The clouds come from a completely different picture – a landscape shot featuring a French château. The building was discarded and just an area of well-defined cloud retained and dropped in behind the subject. The cube shapes and the ball engraved with hearts were drawn on the computer, with the final coloring and shading added to give the final effect of depth and distance.

▷ **This selection of imagery** is presented just to give you a taste of the type of effects you can achieve using modern image-manipulation and 3-D software products. For reference, the (slightly tweaked) original image is presented in the top left-hand corner. The top row is the result of respecifying the colors of the original, while the next two rows will give you some idea of how other images can be combined to give increasingly unrealistic imagery. The final two rows of images have taken the original into the realms of pure imagination.

Using telephoto lenses

You can think of telephoto lenses, also known as long lenses, as being like a telescope. They are ideal when the subject cannot be approached too closely for some reason or when you want to fill the viewfinder with a small subject, or just a small part of a larger one. The longer the lens, the smaller its angle of view – a fact that allows you to concentrate attention on the principal subject by excluding all, or nearly all, of its immediate surroundings. However, telephoto lenses, especially some telephoto zooms, are heavy, and you need to set a fast shutter speed if you are to prevent accidental camera shake spoiling your pictures. With a 250mm lens, for example, you need to use a shutter speed of at least ½50 second. You should not really hand-hold a camera fitted with lenses longer than 250mm– it is better to attach the camera to a tripod or support it in some other way.

Other factors to bear in mind with telephotos is that depth of field will always be limited, even when small apertures are set, which makes accurate focusing even more important than it normally is. As well, telephotos tend to squash the perspective of a scene by enlarging the background in relation to the foreground, and this can be an interesting pictorial device to exploit in some circumstances.

△ **If a standard lens** had been used for this picture, the falling windsurfer would have taken up only a small part of the frame and the large expanse of water would have had little visual appeal or impact.

△ **Storm light toward dusk** has coated the water of this bay with a skin of liquid silver. The angle of view of the 250mm lens used has cropped out most of the rather uninteresting foreground and concentrated the viewer's attention on the silver light and more distant, brooding hills topped with a cloud-choked sky.

◁ **The selective viewpoint** of a telephoto lens has been used to good effect here to include just the heads and upper bodies of this group of African children. Note, too, the isolating effect produced by the limited depth of field.

▷ **Very precise framing** is possible when using a telephoto zoom lens without you having to change camera position – as you would when using a single focal length prime lens. A slightly elevated camera position has recorded none of the sky, which was washed out and featureless and weakened the impact of the desolate buildings below.

△ **A mirror,** or catadioptric, lens is a lightweight type of telephoto. It has a single, fixed aperture, usually about f8, and produces characteristic donut shapes whenever out-of-focus highlights are included in the picture.

◁ **The repeating shapes** of the hills in this photograph, ranked from the foreground through to the horizon, have been accentuated by the perspective-squashing effect of a 300mm telephoto lens. Atmospheric haze also adds to the impression of recession in the picture.

Using wide-angle lenses

Wide-angle lenses come into their own when you are shooting in confined spaces and cannot move very far back from the subject, or when you need to record a broad scene in which the subject is given a proper context. Unlike a telephoto lens (see pp. 174–5), subject elements seen through wide-angles appear diminished in size and more distant than they really are. Rather than enlarging the background in relation to the foreground, wide-angles enlarge the foreground in relation to the background. This is particularly noticeable if they are used very close to, say, a person's face – the forehead and nose, being nearer the lens, look disproportionately large in relation to other parts of the face, such as the chin and ears, which are further away.

Wide-angle lenses in common use range between 24mm and 35mm (for 35mm cameras). Lenses of around 16mm can produce distinct vertical distortion of elements at the frame edges, while 6mm "fisheyes" produce near circular images, taking in a massive 220° of a scene. Depth of field at all apertures is extensive, so much so that when an extreme wide-angle is set at its minimum aperture, depth of field can be so extensive that focusing becomes unnecessary.

◁ **A magnificent vaulted hall,** set for an intimate dinner, has to be photographed with a wide-angle lens if you want to show the splendor of the setting in which the subject has been placed. A telephoto lens would concentrate attention on the figure, using the ornate windows merely as a backdrop.

◁ **Too much depth of field** was my problem when taking this photograph. I had to open up my 28mm lens to f2.8 so that I could imply depth and distance by showing the background figure slightly soft and the foreground pin-sharp.

▷ **A sense of the sky** reaching up and over your head is one of the characteristics associated with wide-angles – and why they are so popular with landscape and cityscape specialists. A polarizing filter was used to increase the contrast between sky and clouds in this scene and to darken the foreground water.

△ ▷ **Horizontal and vertical shots** of a quiet English village were taken from the same spot using a Widelux, which is a type of specialist panoramic camera with a swiveling lens system. As with most panoramic cameras, it is difficult to detect distortions, except in close-ups, although somebody familiar with the scene would notice marked changes in the positions of objects in the field of view of the lens. This type of camera was originally developed for school and other large-group photographs. Subjects positioned in an arc around the camera appear to be in one straight line in the resulting picture, since the lens itself travels in an arc. On a 36-exposure film this camera takes 21 exposures.

Using filters

The value of filters in general photographic work is very limited. However, familiarity with the range that is available and the likely benefits filters bring in enabling you to record colors more accurately under difficult conditions, or to enliven scenes that would otherwise be dull, is invaluable.

Correction filters, which alter the color temperature of light entering the camera to match the type of film being used (see p. 189), form the largest group. Others, including starburst, single color, and dual color, are designed for special effects. Soft-focus filters diffuse the image, and similar results can be achieved by breathing on a plain glass lens filter or lightly smearing it with petroleum jelly (never touch the glass of the lens itself).

Of the correction filters, the most generally useful are skylight and ultraviolet filters, which help to take the blue cast out of shadows and generally "warm-up" the scene. Either can be left on the camera permanently for outdoor photography. Polarizing filters are invaluable for eliminating reflected glare and strengthening the contrast between sky and cloud color. Many filters, however, require some additional exposure since not all pass the same amount of light that falls on them.

△ **A starburst** is a type of diffraction filter that causes small, intense sources of light or bright reflections to flare, forming attractive streaks of light centered on each. Here you see the type of effect you could achieve, but a more distant viewpoint would have shown the stars more obviously.

△ **Warm-up filters** are useful in scenes illuminated principally by a sunless but bright blue sky or, with some types of film in particular, scenes largely in shadow. Requiring no exposure allowance, they give a warmer, sunnier look to images such as this harbor scene, in which colors now appear well balanced.

△ ▷ **Color filters** need to be used judiciously, since the eye quickly tires of seeing artificial coloration in a photograph unless the distortion is somehow motivated by the picture's content. The filter used for the first version of this scene (above) has an overall color, its intensity varying depending on the underlying colors in the scene. The next version (right) shows the use of a graduated filter – the color graduates through progressively lighter shades to clear glass. Twist the filter while it is on the lens, checking its effects through the viewfinder, before you decide how the color should be orientated to suit any particular subject.

△ **A marching band** and a neon-lit street are turned into a glittering cascade of multicolored lights by the combination of two filters. The band is seen in the center of a colorburst filter, which bends light entering the camera into its component parts; the exploding street lighting is the result of adding a starburst filter.

∇ **As well as removing reflections** from some type of polished surfaces, polarizing filters can also be used to add sparkle and drama to pictures. Their main use in color photography is to strengthen the color of blue sky in order to strengthen the contrast between sky and clouds, as is demonstrated in the before and after shots below. Polarizing filters can also be effective in cutting through mist and haze. Twist the filter on the lens to see its effects through the viewfinder.

Equipment and darkroom

Cameras

Cameras for color film are not different from those used in black and white photography and, in general, any piece of equipment capable of producing a sharp picture in one medium will give good results in the other. The very cheapest cameras, however, in addition to producing images with detail less-critically sharp, will not be able to register colors correctly.

All cameras have a lens that forms an image on light-sensitive material. They also have a shutter for controlling the length of time light is allowed to act on the film, and an aperture, which determines the quantity, or intensity, of light entering the lens. The versatility of cameras and the character and quality of the images they produce vary enormously. But a basic way of

categorizing them is in terms of the size of film they use and their method of focusing (see also pp. 184–5).

FILM SIZES

The most widely used film size is, by far, 35mm. Transparencies in this film size are large enough to project onto screens without loss of quality, and prints from 35mm negatives look good even when considerably enlarged. 35mm film is packed in convenient cassettes containing 24 or 36 frames, and film loading is virtually automatic on most modern cameras.

Although most photographers use 35mm film, so-called professional cameras, known as medium format cameras, take a larger size of film called 120 or 220 rollfilm, depending on the number of frames it contains. The actual number of frames depends on the camera type, since the term "medium format" encompasses three popular images sizes (see opposite). Rollfilm is less convenient to load than 35mm, but its larger image size gives finer, better-quality results, especially when images are projected or enlarged to a great degree. These cameras are also, in general, less automated and slower to use than 35mm types.

CAMERA TYPES

Dividing up cameras by film type is a useful way to gain a broad view of their physical dimensions and capabilities, but in order to obtain an idea of how they handle in practice, it is necessary to look briefly at other factors – the most important of these being the way the photographer both views and focuses the image formed by the camera.

Found on 35mm compact cameras and some medium format models is a system known as direct-vision viewing. Although cumbersome to use, it does allow the camera to be less heavy and bulky and so it is popular. In effect, these cameras have a separate window through which you look to compose the image. The viewfinder – which is constructed much like a back-to-front telescope – shows approximately what the lens will record.

Reflex cameras give an extremely accurate view of what the lens will record, since the photographer sees on

▷ **For serious photography** the 35mm SLR is the smallest camera format to use. The lens can be removed and any of the whole range from the camera maker or independents put in it place. The pentaprism shape on top houses a mirror system that directs light from the lens to the eyepiece.

▷ **The 6 x 6cm camera** (also known as a 2¼in square camera) is probably the best known of the rollfilm formats, being the oldest and best established of its type. This camera produces square negatives or slides.

◁ **35mm compacts,** also known as point-and-shoot cameras, are the most popular type with amateur photographers. This model has built-in flash, an impressive zoom lens, and a high degree of automation.

◁ **The 6 x 4.5cm rollfilm camera** is the smallest of the medium-format cameras, but the film image it produces is still substantially larger than that from a 35mm camera (see opposite).

◁ **The 6 x 7cm camera** is the largest of the popular rollfilm formats – although a 6 x 9cm model is also available. The large area of the film originals it produces means that you get fewer exposures per roll of film, making more frequent film changes necessary.

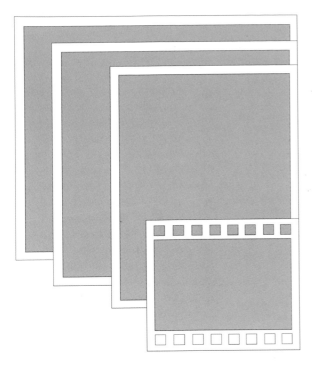

◁ **Shown actual size** are the film sizes for the four most popular camera formats. The smallest film is made for 35mm cameras – compacts and SLRs. This film has sprocket holes that engage with special spools inside the camera to advance it one frame at a time. The next largest is 6 x 4.5cm rollfilm, then 6 x 6cm, and finally 6 x 7cm. These three rollfilms are all based on the same format (they share a common dimension) but, depending on the camera they are used in, a different length of film is exposed each time. Rollfilm does not have sprocket holes and it comes packed with a special backing paper that is rolled back as the film advances through the camera.

SYSTEM CAMERAS

Any single camera, however well designed, is inevitably a compromise and cannot be expected to meet the needs of every photographer. Therefore, most manufacturers, particularly of 35mm SLR cameras, produce a system of additional lenses and accessories. Generally, lenses and accessories are dedicated to just one brand of camera, or even to just one or two top-of-the-range models within that brand. Independent makers produce adaptors to provide a limited amount of interchangeability between brands, but with the increasing complexity of electronic cameras, such items are becoming extremely difficult to engineer.

Much of the versatility of the system SLR arises from the choice of lenses (see pp. 186–8), ranging from extreme wide-angle fisheyes to powerful telephotos. All modern system cameras have an integral film advance, so a separate motor drive is no longer necessary. However, the built-in motor is powerful enough only to advance conventional cassettes of 35mm film, and most bulk film backs have their own motor.

The advent of autofocus has rendered elaborate focusing accessories largely obsolete, but a few system cameras still have interchangeable viewfinders with higher magnifications or special metering features. And interchangeable focusing screens provide further choice of viewing options.

the focusing screen the actual image produced by the lens.

Most reflex cameras have a single lens; an internal mirror throws the image from the lens onto a matt screen so that focusing and viewing are precise and accurate. Just before exposure occurs, the mirror flips up (temporarily blanking out the viewfinder), allowing the light from the lens to travel to the back of the camera, where a shutter opens to reveal the surface of the film. These cameras, 35mm or medium format, are called single lens reflex (SLR) cameras.

Twin lens reflex (TLR) cameras operate in a similar manner, but they have a fixed mirror behind a second lens (ranked above the first), which is used exclusively for viewing and composition. The main, or taking, lens is used purely for making the image on the film, not for viewing the subject. Changing lenses on this type of medium-format camera involves changing the viewing and taking lenses, which are on a single panel. TLRs share the same problem as direct-vision cameras – you do not see precisely the same image as that taken in by the lens.

ADVANCE PHOTO SYSTEM (APS)

The newest camera and film format to be launched is the advanced photo system (APS), and is a collaborative venture by the leading camera and film producers. Despite having a smaller film size than 35mm (and smaller, lighter cameras), APS emulsion gives about the same print quality. The APS cassette is considerably easier to load, since all you need do is drop it in to the film compartment and then leave the rest to the camera, making mistakes impossible.

The real difference between APS and other types of camera is that you can select from three different picture formats before taking the shot. The C (classic) setting mimics the familiar 35mm shape; the H setting gives you a wider format; while for the extra-wide setting, select P (panoramic). Although the whole film area is exposed each time, your format selection is registered on a magnetic coating included on the

film that communicates with the processing machine (in a process known as information exchange, or IX), which crops the image accordingly. As well as recording format information, the film also registers exposure data, which again is passed on to the processing machine to help improve image quality. Another useful feature of the APS system is that you can change film partway through a roll. Rewind the film and then, when you load the cassette back into the camera, it winds forward until it reaches the next frame to be exposed.

DIGITAL CAMERAS

Digital cameras are radically different from conventional stills cameras in that instead of using film to record images, they use a CCD (charge-coupled device). A CCD consists of thousands of tiny light-sensitive pixels, which produce an electrical output in direct proportion to the amount of light falling on them. In

△ Advance photo system camera

▽ Digital camera

this way, the camera builds up an electronic map of the subject, which can be output to film or paper if a slide or print is required, or downloaded directly into a computer.

Focusing methods

◁ **With a close-up subject** you need to pay particular attention to the framing lines in the viewfinder of a direct-vision camera. These guidelines are usually accurate for more distant subjects, but it is easy to cut off, say, part of the head of a person positioned nearby.

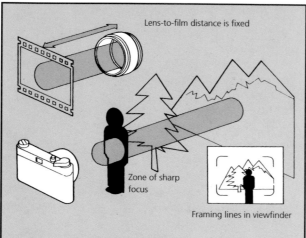

Lens-to-film distance is fixed

Zone of sharp focus

Framing lines in viewfinder

◁ **With a fixed-focus camera** the lens-to-film distance is fixed, and a usefully deep zone of acceptably sharp focus (known as the depth of field) is achieved by the use of a small working aperture and a moderate wide-angle lens. The direct-vision viewfinder on this type of camera may have framing lines to aid composition. These guides tend to be least accurate with close-up subjects.

▷ **Rangefinder focusing** is preferred by some photographers because it is quick and very positive, and as the system does not need a reflex mirror, cameras are very quiet. An arrangement of cams moves a system of prisms within the viewfinder (1), so that the photographer, in effect, views the subject through two windows. Focusing (2) brings the two views together in the viewfinder.

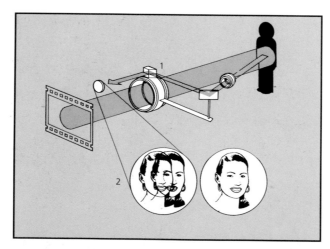

▷ **Reflex viewing** is the most accurate for viewing and composition. An angled mirror (1) inside the camera body reflects light from the lens up to a focusing screen (2) and pentaprism (3), where the still laterally reversed image is corrected, left-to-right, before being viewed through the eyepiece (4). For exposure, the mirror flips up before the shutter opens.

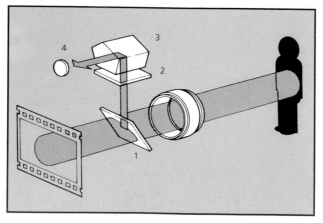

The simplest of cameras have lens and film rigidly arranged at a fixed distance apart. Theoretically, these cameras form sharp images only of subjects at one fixed distance, so they are often referred to as "fixed-focus" cameras. In practice, however, the lenses of fixed-focus cameras are moderately wide-angle and have a small working aperture, a combination that produces a broad depth of field, and so, within limits, everything appears reasonably sharp. Such cameras give acceptable pictures in bright, sunny conditions outdoors, and because they lack a focusing mechanism they are robust and inexpensive to make. However, they lack versatility, cannot take sharp pictures of nearby subjects, and focusing is always approximate, never precise.

VARIABLE FOCUS

To focus with accuracy, the lens must be able to move in relation to the film, to bring into focus closer and more distant subjects. Scale-focusing cameras have simple calibrations on the lens to indicate which parts of the scene will be sharp on the film. Typically, the lens rotates in a threaded collar so that it moves in and out as it is turned. The closer the lens is to the film plane, the sharper more distant subjects become; moving it further away from the film plane focuses the lens on closer subjects. Distance markings, or symbols, engraved on the lens barrel show where the lens should be positioned for optimum sharpness. Focusing accuracy is limited, though, by the photographer's ability to guess subject distances.

A more reliable way to focus is to monitor subject sharpness directly by throwing the image from the lens onto a focusing screen. To achieve this, the popular SLR uses a mirror directly behind the lens to direct the image from the lens upward, where it can be viewed through the eyepiece at the back of the camera. For this system to work, the distance from the mirror to the focusing screen must be the same as the distance between the mirror and the film plane.

THE COUPLED RANGEFINDER

The reflex viewing system used in SLRs is an elegant solution to the problem of achieving well-focused images, but there are other, equally effective, answers. The Leica and its imitators have a rangefinder coupled to the movement of the lens. As the camera is focused, the photographer sees in the direct-vision viewfinder a double image of the subject. The act of turning the lens to focus brings the two images together, until they merge at the point of sharpest focus.

Rangefinders are mechanically less complex than SLRs and have few moving parts. They lack the hinged mirror of the SLR and so are almost silent in operation. Some photographers prefer the coupled rangefinder because they feel that its method of focusing is more positive and precise than reflex focusing, especially when working in dim lighting and with wide-angle lenses.

AUTOMATIC FOCUSING

On sophisticated modern cameras, all functions, including focusing, are accomplished automatically. Autofocus mechanisms work in one of two ways, and they are described as being either active or passive.

Active autofocus systems are usually built into compact point-and-shoot 35mm cameras, and they work by utilizing a beam of infrared light to measure the distance to the subject. This approach performs well if the camera has a fixed lens and it is inexpensive to manufacture. There are some situations, however, that can lead active autofocus systems into error – shiny or very dark surfaces, for example, reflect or absorb the beam of infrared light, leading to incorrect focus. As well, infrared will be reflected by, say, a pane of glass, which makes shooting through a glass window problematic.

Passive autofocus systems have much more in common with manual reflex focusing – an electronic sensor simply replaces the human eye as a means of judging sharpest focus. They work by relying on the fact that sharply focused objects have more contrast than unsharp ones. Thus, they move the lens in and out until maximum contrast is registered, and then stop. This system runs into trouble, however, when you are trying to focus on subjects that have inherently low contrast or when focusing on flatly lit, same-color subjects with little surface information – exactly the same subjects that would cause problems when focusing manually. These systems are incorporated in all the most recent 35mm SLRs, and the technology has become extremely sophisticated.

It seems very likely that in the near future either active or passive autofocus systems will be a part of all but very cheap or highly specialized cameras.

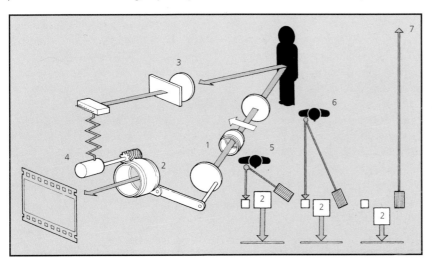

△ **Active autofocus** is activated when you depress the shutter release. A beam of infrared (1) shines toward the subject and starts the lens (2) moving, to focus on progressively greater distances. As the lens moves, the beam of infrared (IR) sweeps across the subject, its scanning motion synchronized with that of the lens. A forward-pointing infrared sensor (3) detects when the beam has struck the subject, indicating that the lens is focused. The sensor then instructs the camera's microprocessor to stop the lens motor (4) and, if the shutter release has been fully depressed, to open the shutter. A beam strikes a close subject (5) quickly and the lens stops before it is very close to the film. With a middle-distance subject (6), the lens is driven closer. No IR echo is received from far subjects (7), so the lens focuses on infinity.

▷ **Passive autofocus** is the system found on SLR cameras. The passive system of autofocus employs a tiny mirror (1) hanging behind a semi-transparent section of the main reflex mirror. This small mirror "steals" some of the viewfinder image for focusing purposes. The image is then divided into two, and each half is reflected onto a sensor (2) in the base of the camera. Signals from the sensor are analyzed by the camera's circuits (3), and the focusing motor is activated to move the lens until the peak signals from the two sensors coincide (4), indicating that the picture will be sharp. This system of autofocus works on the principle that sharply focused subjects are more contrasty than out-of-focus ones.

◁ **One problem** encountered by users of autofocus is that some systems assume that the subject to be focused on is positioned in certain parts of the frame – often the middle. A very off-center subject, such as this jumping figure, might be ignored by the autofocus, and the lens set on infinity instead.

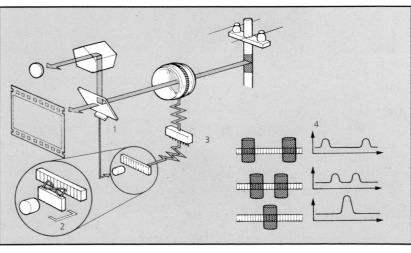

Lenses

No single lens is as adaptable as the lens of the human eye (see pp. 20–1). But there are specific lenses that can record more detail than the unaided eye can perceive. Selecting the appropriate lens and using it to full advantage is possible only if certain optical characteristics are properly understood.

FOCAL LENGTH

When choosing a lens, a photographer has to know its focal length – the distance behind a lens at which a sharp image will be formed when the lens is focused at infinity (marked ∞ on the focusing scale) – and the effect it will have on the image. The longer the focal length the larger will be the image size. If, for example, a 50mm lens produces a 3mm image of an object, a 100mm lens will produce a 6mm image of the same subject. In doing so, the 100mm lens will reduce the total area of the scene proportionally. On the other hand, a 25mm lens will include a greater area of a scene but on a smaller scale.

By convention, a "normal", or "standard", lens is one with a focal length approximately equal to the diagonal of the format of the film it covers. On 35mm film, which measures 24 x 36mm, the diagonal is about 45mm. Thus, lenses with focal lengths in the region between 45mm and 55mm are described as standard.

The diagonal of 6 x 6cm (2¼in square) rollfilm is about 85mm, and so lenses between 75mm and 90mm are considered standard for that particular format. Lenses shorter than the standard focal length are designated as wide-angle lenses, while those with longer focal lengths are called telephoto lenses. Therefore, an 85mm lens used with 35mm film would be considered a telephoto, while a 50mm lens used with 6 x 6cm film would be a wide-angle.

CHOICE OF LENSES

Most subjects can be recorded with a selection of three prime lenses – a moderate wide-angle (28–35mm on a 35mm camera), a standard lens (45–55mm), and a medium telephoto lens (90–135mm). There will be times, however, when you may need a special-purpose lens to extend the image-recording ability of your camera.

With cameras that have interchangeable lenses it is possible to take extreme close-ups by increasing the distance between the lens and the film with bellows attachments or extension tubes. Macro lenses are also available for working at very close distances and can record images that are on the same scale as the objects they photograph.

Very wide-angle lenses are difficult to design, one of the problems being the effects of distortion. Fisheye lenses, which can have angles of view as wide as 220°, attempt to make a virtue of distortion by producing circular pictures with straight lines appearing as concentric curves. The effect can be dramatic, but few subjects suit this type of treatment or warrant the expense of the lens.

Shift lenses are wide-angle lenses, made primarily for 35mm cameras, that can be moved off their normal axis in order to provide a certain degree of control over perspective. The results are similar to those obtainable on a view camera with swinging and rising front controls. They are most widely used in architectural photography, particularly to encompass tall buildings without the sides of the structure appearing to converge as they would with an ordinary lens tilted upward.

Zoom lenses are useful for their variable focal lengths. Once the subject is in focus, focal length can be changed at will to alter the scale of the image. Most zoom lenses have 13 or more elements and are, consequently, heavier, and more expensive, than any comparable lens of fixed focal length. But two zooms will still be less expensive and lighter than a set of, say, five separate prime lenses that covers the same range of focal lengths. For 35mm cameras, zoom lenses with variable focal lengths between 28mm and 210mm are most useful. Those with longer focal lengths tend to be too heavy for hand-held photography, while high-quality, wide-angle zooms are difficult to make. Many zoom lenses can be locked in at a macro setting, giving yet a further dimension to an already versatile lens.

ADAPTORS AND CONVERTERS

One way to provide a single camera lens with wide-angle or telephoto capability is by fitting adaptor lenses. They usually

allow for an increase or decrease of only one-third of the focal length of the lens to which they are attached, a change many photographers may consider negligible. Converter lenses, however, can actually double or treble the focal length of a lens. Fitted between the camera body and the lens, converters work by magnifying the center of the image formed by the existing lens.

Converters are most often used with telephoto lenses. You may, for example, have a 250mm lens and consider that a 500mm lens would be too heavy, too expensive, or used too seldom to be worth having. By fitting a 2x converter, however, you can effectively double the focal length of your 250mm lens and achieve results comparable with those of a separate 500mm lens. But there are disadvantages in using converters – they decrease the amount of light reaching the film, they increase the likelihood of flare, and they may also reduce image contrast unless made with good-quality, coated glass elements.

△ ▽ **100mm telephoto** Lenses of this focal length are often described as portrait lenses, since you can fill the frame with a head-and-shoulders shot without approaching too close to the subject, and the perspective created by this focal length is generally flattering to the face. As you can see from the image below, it is also ideal for isolating detail in more distant landscapes. This lens is not heavy and so can be safely hand-held at even quite slow shutter speeds if care is taken in camera handling.

△ ▽ **15mm extreme wide-angle** The wide angle of view of a lens such as this makes it ideal for landscape shots in which there is plenty of interest and detail in all areas of the frame. Although it encompasses a broad swathe of the landscape, no particular feature in the image below can be said to be the main point of interest, since all detail appears very distant and diminished. The depth of field of extreme wide-angles is extensive at all apertures, which is useful for masking minor focusing errors.

△ ▽ **28mm wide-angle** This focal length is probably the most generally useful wide-angle lens. Taking in a 74° angle of view, it is suitable for broad landscape subjects, but since edge distortion (bowing of vertical lines at the sides of the frame) is not normally a problem, except on poorly made budget lenses, it has many other applications as well.

△ ▽ **50mm standard lens** This focal length lens used to be normally supplied with 35mm SLR camera bodies, but it is now often replaced with a zoom encompassing 50mm. The principal advantages to a prime 50mm lens are: weight, this type of lens is far lighter than a zoom lens; optical quality, standard lenses will often resolve more subject detail than a zoom lens set to 50mm; and speed, standard lenses are often the fastest (have the largest maximum aperture) of any lens in a manufacturer's range.

△ ▽ **200mm telephoto** This is about the longest focal length that is suitable for general photography. Its angle of view is becoming restricted and so it is ideal for pulling distant subjects up large in the viewfinder, but its weight is starting to increase to the point where it can be safely hand-held only at brief shutter speeds, such as 1/250 second and briefer. Since these lenses are also quite slow (often about f4–f5.6), shutter speeds as brief as this are only possible in very good lighting.

△ ▽ **300mm telephoto** This type of focal length is probably going to be of more interest to the specialist photographer – perhaps somebody involved in, say, wildlife photography, or if you want to pick out a single face from a crowd of people. These lenses are also very slow, unless you are prepared to spend a lot of money, and heavy, requiring the use of shutter speeds that require a tripod or some other type of support. This lens incorporates a tripod-mounting collar for this purpose.

△ ▽ **500mm mirror** The different appearance of this extreme telephoto is due to the fact that some of the conventional glass elements, or lenses, within the lens barrel have been replaced by lightweight mirrors. The mirrors bounce the light up and down, effectively giving you a long telephoto in a physically short barrel. The major drawback with mirror lenses is that they have only a single working aperture, usually f8. This severely restricts them to good lighting conditions, even when fast film is being used.

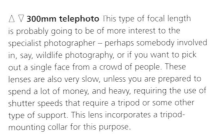

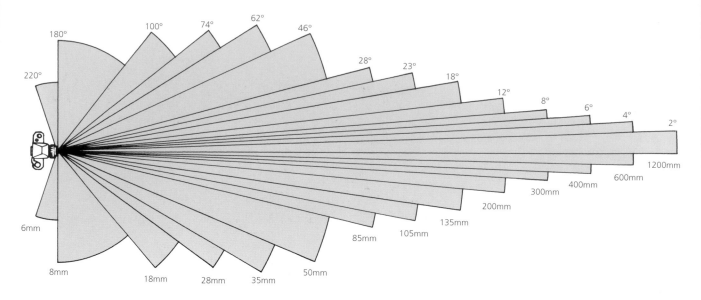

MIRROR LENSES

Telephoto lenses are, of course, used for photographing distant subjects, or just small parts of subjects that are positioned closer to the camera (bearing in mind the minimum focusing distance of these lenses), but their limited depth of field (see box below) also makes them excellent for isolating a subject from its background. Accurately focused and at maximum aperture, a telephoto lens can pick out one face from a blurred crowd of people. But, generally, the longer the lens the heavier it is, and some can be used only if they are mounted on a sturdy tripod, or firmly supported in some other way. To overcome the problems of size and weight associated with using telephoto, lens manufacturers devised catadioptric, or mirror, lenses. These use a combination of internal lenses and mirrored surfaces to reflect light backward and forward inside the lens barrel so that focal length is, as it were, folded up. As a result, the physical length of mirror lenses can be much reduced and, by substituting mirrors for some internal lenses, weight is also dramatically reduced. One drawback, however, is that the f number is fixed, usually at f8.

ANGLE OF VIEW

Another factor when understanding the work you want lenses to do is their angle of view – that is, the amount of the scene that is encompassed by a particular focal length (see diagram above). A standard lens, irrespective of the film size, has an angle of view of between 45° and 55°. Telephoto lenses take in angles of view of 30° down to only 2°, while wide-angle lenses have angles of view in excess of 60°

F NUMBER SCALE

The amount of light reaching the film is controlled by an iris diaphragm, which can be opened up to allow in more light or closed down to restrict it. The size of the diaphragm's aperture is important not only because it affects exposure times but also because it determines, to some extent, the depth of field.

The aperture is measured in f numbers (or f stops), which range from a maximum opening of f1 or larger to a minimum opening of perhaps f64 or smaller, with intermediate stops of 1.4, 2, 2.8, 4, 5.6, 8, 11, 16, 22, 32, and 45. When stopping down, each f number allows in half the light of the preceding one and twice as much light as the one following. For example, f2 will allow half as much light through the lens as f1.4 and a quarter of the light of f1, but twice the light of f2.8 and four times the light of f4. Intermediate stops, such as 1.2, 1.8, or 3.5, can also be selected.

DEPTH OF FIELD

When a lens is focused at a specific distance, only objects at that distance are recorded with maximum sharpness, although objects both in front of and behind that point may be acceptably sharp. The zone between the closest and furthest points of acceptably sharp focus is known as the *depth of field*.

Three factors determine the depth of field – the focal length of the lens, the aperture (or f number) selected, and the camera-to-subject distance. Depth of field *increases* as the focal length of the lens becomes shorter, as the aperture is stopped down (gets smaller), and as the camera-to-subject distance becomes greater. It *decreases* with lenses of longer focal length, when larger apertures are selected, and when the subject in focus is closer to the camera.

Most camera lenses have depth-of-field scales engraved on them, but these are worked out on the basis of a predetermined degree of picture enlargement. The scale engraved on lenses made for 35mm cameras, for example, may be relevant for a print size of 8½ x 6½in (21.6 x 16.5cm). If larger prints than this are made, then the depth of field will be less than that indicated on the scale, and with smaller prints the depth of field will be greater than that indicated. It is important to note that depth of field does not begin and end abruptly, but it changes gradually from a blur to acceptable sharpness, and also that the notion of what is, or is not, thought of as "acceptably" sharp is a highly subjective one.

Nearly all lenses improve in their performance when they are stopped down to smaller apertures. A 50mm lens at f2, for example, would increase in sharpness, especially toward the edges of the picture, when stopped down to f5.6 or f8. At very small apertures, however, such as f16 or f22 with the same lens, the narrower aperture would begin diffracting light, causing some fall-off in subject definition. The longer the focal length of the lens, the greater the f number permissible before the problem of diffraction begins to arise.

Filters

Although color films are balanced for particular light sources, such as daylight, electronic flash, or tungsten, they can be used with other sources if appropriate correcting filters are used.

The colors of light sources, natural and artificial, are described in terms of color temperature, measured in kelvins (see pp. 16–17). With color slide film, matching the film to the color temperature of the light source is crucial, since there is no stage between exposing the film and processing the final image at which corrections can be made. This is why there are two types of slide film available: daylight (balanced for about 5,500K, which corresponds to midday sunlight and the light from electronic flash) and tungsten (balanced for approximately 3,200K, which corresponds to the color temperature of tungsten-halogen lighting).

Unless corrected by filters, the mismatching of these films and their recommended light sources will produce slides with varying color casts. Daylight-balanced film, for example, exposed under artificial lighting will have a warm orange cast (because tungsten light is blue deficient), while tungsten-balanced film exposed in daylight will produce slides with a distinct blue cast (because the film has been produced to

Using color-correcting filters

Light source	Film type	Color cast if unfiltered	Filter correction	Increase in f stop
Tungsten halogen	Tungsten	None	None	None
	Daylight	Orange	80A	2
Noon daylight	Tungsten	Strong blue	85B	⅔
(or electronic flash)	Daylight	None	None	None
Photofloods	Daylight	Yellow/orange	80B	1⅔

compensate for blue-deficient tungsten, a problem that does not exist in daylight).

Color negative films are nearly all balanced for the approximate color temperature of daylight. Even if they are exposed under artificial tungsten light, any resulting color casts can be mostly corrected at the printing stage.

Using fluorescent light for photography can be problematic because many fluorescent tubes emit an incomplete spectrum, which, although not obvious to the human eye, will appear as a greenish color cast on daylight-balanced slide films. Using an FL-D filter may help to minimize the cast, but the degree of correction is dependent on the type of tube, so you will need to experiment to determine the filter's effectiveness.

Some filters can be used not only for color correction but also for the dramatic and artistic control of color (see

pp. 180–1). A blue filter, for example, used with daylight film might be used to convey a feeling a coldness or to simulate moonlight, while some filters have a single color of varying density to allow you to color some parts of a scene (a pale, featureless sky, perhaps) and leave others parts (the land) unaltered. But bear in mind that all colored filters reduce the total amount of light reaching the film. This means that you then have to use either a larger lens aperture or a slower shutter speed (or both). The stronger the filter color, the greater the light loss.

Color-correcting filters are made by a number of different manufacturers and all use different codes to denote their effects. Those in the chart above are widely available examples, but there is no necessarily obvious connection between the coding used by manufacturers and their filters' effects.

◁ ▽ **Tungsten-balanced film** used to photograph a scene illuminated by daylight (left) produces this obvious blue cast. With the appropriate color-correction filter over the lens, however, casts can be largely removed and true colors restored (below).

◁ ▽ **Daylight-balanced film** will produce this over-warm orange cast (left) if it is exposed in domestic (tungsten) lighting. If you don't want to use flash, which is balanced for the temperature of daylight, a correction filter will restore color balance (below).

Supports and lights

The flexibility of the camera increases markedly when you have accessories such as camera supports and supplementary lights. These will allow you to tackle low-light scenes, wildlife photography, and a whole range of special effects. However, equipment such as this is useful only if you are thoroughly familiar with its operation and that you make proper use of it. Too much choice can lead to delay and missed photographic opportunities.

SUPPORTS

Camera supports are used in order to prevent camera shake and to fix the camera's position so that all of the photographer's attention can be concentrated on composition and deciding precisely when to make the exposure. Generally, cameras fitted with wide-angle and standard lenses can be hand-held at shutter speeds down to about ½₀ second before the effects of vibration can be detected in a picture. With telephoto lenses, however, vibration will be more noticeable. When shooting with long lenses some photographers use a tripod if their shutter speed becomes longer than ½₅₀ second.

Much depends on how firm your grip is on the camera. Very large and bulky cameras – or for that matter very small and lightweight cameras – are difficult to hold steadily. The stability of the photographer's stance and the way the camera is held may also determine whether or not a tripod, or some other form of support, should be used. A camera held at waist level, for example, shakes less than one held at eye level because the effects of body sway increase from the feet upward. To counter this, make your body as stable a platform as possible by standing in a relaxed fashion, with your weight distributed equally over both legs, and with boths hand supporting the cameras. Breathe in and hold just as you are about to press the shutter release and press lightly on the shutter button – jabbing downward on it will inevitably jar the camera.

The most stable supports are those used in film and television studios, where steadiness is more important than portability. These are far too heavy to lift, so they are mounted on castors or wheeled trollies. At the other extreme are table-top tripods that can fit into a generous pocket. These are useful when you want to use a wall, or something similar, to support the camera for, say, a manually timed night exposure but want a perfectly level and steady image. A table-top tripod is not really suitable for a camera fitted with a heavy long lens, since the weight at the front may tip the tripod forward.

A good compromise is an aluminum alloy tripod with lockable, extending legs. This type of tripod usually has a center column that can be raised or lowered for rapid height adjustment.

Although tripods provide the best type of camera support, they are not suitable in all situations. Where space is tight, for example, or in crowded street scenes you might need to use a more compact support such as a monopod. Alternatively pistol-grips and rifle-grips help to steady the camera, giving sharper pictures at slow shutter speeds than would otherwise be possible.

LIGHTS

In many indoor situations – purpose-built studios and more informal indoor settings – natural daylight plays an important part in photography, both as the principal light source and as fill-in used in association with other sources. The quantity of window light can be regulated with opaque blinds, while its quality can be softened by using different weights of tracing paper over the glass.

Illumination from ordinary domestic light bulbs may seem bright to the naked eye, but it is inadequate, in terms of color temperature, for most color photography. Instead, tungsten filament lamps can be used. These are the same in principle as the domestic varieties, but have greatly enhanced light output. Tungsten lamps are inexpensive to buy, but their bulbs have a very short

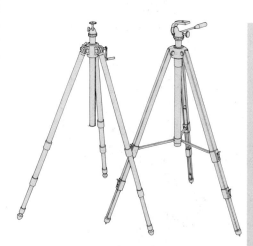

△ **There is always a trade-off** between portability and stability with tripods – there is no point buying one that is so heavy you never take it out. For added rigidity, some tripods have struts joining the legs and center column. Look for smoothness of operation of all the tripod controls and how easily the tripod head can be locked and unlocked, and the camera platform turned on its side for portrait-format shots.

TRIPOD HEADS

Photographers who depend on always taking critically sharp pictures, the quality of the tripod head is crucial. Heads can be bought separately from the tripod itself, and some hydraulic heads are so precisely engineered they can cost much more than even a good-quality camera. There is, however, a wide range of heads to suit every need and budget.
1 A simple ball-and-socket head rotates in all directions and tilts up and down. Control with this type of head is basic.
2 Two-way heads are a step up in sophistication. All movement is controlled by twisting the handle to lock and unlock the head.
3 The most versatile type of tripod head is a three-way pan-and-tilt type. The camera platform can also be turned on its side.

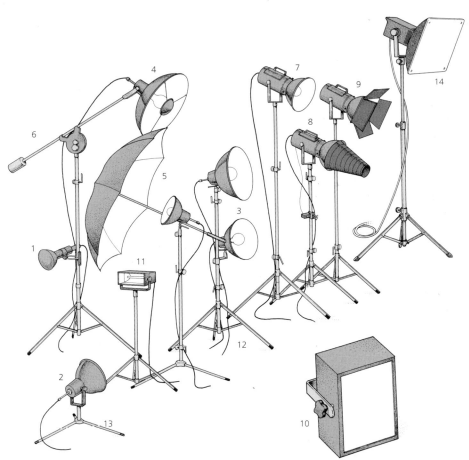

Studio lighting units

1 The bare bulb of a photoflood produces a hard type of light. This can be modified by directing the beam onto a wall or ceiling so that only reflected light reaches the subject.
2 A small, deep reflector bowl helps to direct the light, but it still produces hard shadows.
3 Large, shallow reflector bowls provide a slightly softer lighting effect.
4 A broad reflector bowl can be fitted with a small central shield to block direct light from the bulb so that the effect is that of diffused illumination.
5 An umbrella, or brolly, reflector produces light with a generally soft appearance. Lighting quality varies depending on the material of the brolly itself.
6 A boom arm helps you to position lighting heads precisely, especially when the stand itself cannot be placed too close to the subject.
7 A studio flash unit provides more output than a tungsten bulb and can be used with daylight-balanced film.
8 This flash head is fitted with a snoot to produce a very accurate, narrow beam of light.
9 Barndoors limit the amount of light coming from the sides of the head.
10 Fluorescent tubes in a light box can be used if they have been balanced for daylight output.
11 Tungsten-halogen lamps have a longer working life than ordinary tungsten, and color is more stable.
12 Lighting stands allow you to position a light anywhere and adjust its height.
13 A short lighting stand can be useful for small subjects when low-level lighting is needed.
14 A softbox attachment fits around the lighting head and has a diffusing panel in the front.

operating life and so constant replacement costs could make them more expensive in the long run. The bulbs also generate large amounts of heat, which can be uncomfortable to work under. On the plus side, tungsten lamps do not require synchronization leads and their constant light output makes it easy to judge the final effects of any lighting scheme as you can see precisely where shadows and highlights are falling.

The other main form of artificial photographic light comes from electronic flash. Studio units are mains powered, have near instantaneous recycling times, and their output can be controlled in 1-stop and ½-stop increments. Depending on the precise circumstances of the studio, flash duration can be astonishingly fast, making it ideal for "action-stopping" shots, and the color temperature of flash matches that of daylight, so both can be mixed in the same shot without color cast becoming a factor. All flash, however, has to be synchronized to the camera's shutter. In a multi-light set-up, only one has to be cabled to the camera; the others can be triggered with slave units. Built-in modeling lights allow you to see the fall of light and shade before exposure.

ACCESSORY FLASH

Like electronic studio flash, the illumination from accessory flash units has the same color temperature as daylight. They can thus be used indoors or outdoors as the principal light source or as fill-in when natural light levels are too low or contrast is too harsh. Another major advantage of accessory flash is its portability.

The power source for these units is batteries. As you know from using a torch, when batteries are fresh light output is high, but this diminishes as the batteries wear out. With flash, a capacitor ensures that flash output is consistent, but flash recycling times become progressively longer. To overcome this, some units can be attached to a heavy-duty battery pack worn on a belt around the photographer's waist. A fully charged pack will give hundreds of flashes, depending on subject distance and the reflective qualities of the surroundings. A dedicated unit is designed to be used with a specific camera, integrating with its exposure circuitry to ensure that the appropriate amount of light is delivered.

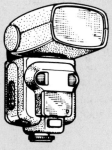

△ **Mounted in the camera hot shoe,** this type of flash points directly at the subject. To allow for a greater range of effects, the flash head swivels to the side or tilts upward so that bounced illumination from the walls or ceiling reaches the subject.

△ **Mounted on the side of the camera** by a metal bar that screws into the tripod bush, this type of accessory flash also has a tilt-and-swivel head. The stem of the flash accommodates large batteries or you can use it with a heavy-duty battery pack.

Darkroom layout and equipment

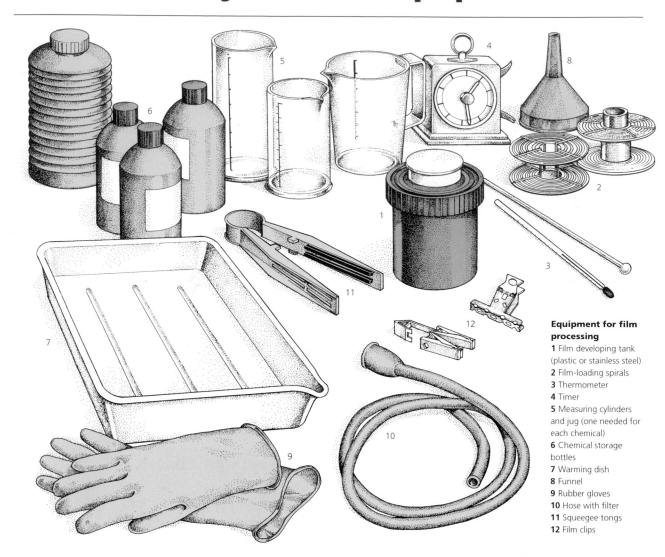

Equipment for film processing
1 Film developing tank (plastic or stainless steel)
2 Film-loading spirals
3 Thermometer
4 Timer
5 Measuring cylinders and jug (one needed for each chemical)
6 Chemical storage bottles
7 Warming dish
8 Funnel
9 Rubber gloves
10 Hose with filter
11 Squeegee tongs
12 Film clips

You can best plan an efficient darkroom by considering the flow of work in terms of step-by-step sequences, and then organizing the equipment accordingly within the available space.

The basic requirement is to exclude all outside light. Windows can be covered with overlapping black felt curtains or purpose-built black-out blinds. Then decide where specific jobs will be done in the room. Consider any part of the room where chemicals or water will be used as the "wet" area and separate it from the "dry" area, where enlarging and related tasks will be carried out (see opposite). All work surfaces should be resistant to chemicals, free from cracks or joins, and easily cleanable. A heavy, firmly supported bench should be used to support the enlarger.

The safest way to handle color materials is in total darkness. Although certain materials can be used with safelights, these do not give out enough light to be really useful. Color prints can

be processed in open dishes or in a light-tight print drum, which allows you to work in normal room lights once the print is safely inside. Films are processed in light-tight tanks, made either of stainless steel or plastic, and you will also need a precision timer for all processing and printing stages, and an accurate thermometer for testing the chemicals at each stage of the process.

CHOOSING AN ENLARGER
Most of the equipment for printing from color negatives or transparencies is the same as that used for black and white, but in any darkroom set up specifically for color printing, a color enlarger is by far the biggest investment. While any black and white enlarger fitted with a filter drawer is suitable, enlargers with special color heads carrying dial-in filters are more effective and easier to use.

Choose an enlarger with a column as long and as rigid as possible. Even if you don't want to make giant enlargements,

there will be times when you want to make a large print from just part of a negative or transparency, and so you will need the enlarger head at the top of the column. Examine the positions of controls, such as the column lock and and focusing knob, and make sure they are well placed and easy to use.

Negative carriers hold the film in the enlarger. Some have glass inserts to prevent the film curling. However, these provide four extra surfaces on which dust can collect and are not recommended. The size of the baseboard should correspond to the largest size of print you are likely to make. Choose a print easel with adjustable borders and clearly marked scales.

METERS AND ANALYZERS
The two critical factors in the initial stages of producing a color print are exposure and color balance. You can measure exposure using a printing meter, which can either take spot readings from

a small area of the projected image, or integrated (average) readings from the unfocused light just beneath the enlarger lens. An analyzer measures the color balance. It, too, can take either spot or integrated readings. The information is translated into a set of numbers on a metered scale or digital display that is used for determining the mix of filters dialled into the head.

PROCESSING CHEMICALS

Chemical kits containing crystals, powder, or concentrated liquid are available for processing a number of films and prints. Unless otherwise indicated, only the process recommended on the film cassette, the outer wrapper of roll film, or the packet of printing paper should be followed. Many types of color film and paper are available, and developers, bleaches, and baths, while formulated to do similar jobs, are designed primarily for a specific manufacturer's products.

All color chemicals conform to rigid safety standards, but you must still handle them with care. Read the instructions carefully. Some chemicals can cause minor skin or eye irritation, but apart from this, badly prepared chemicals will lead to processing faults that can ruin films and prints.

The most common processing fault is chemical contamination. To prevent chemicals coming into contact with each other, keep your working area clean. And always mix chemicals in their order of use – developer first, then bleach, and so on. As a rule, less harm is caused if contamination is from a preceding chemical in the process rather than a following one. Bleach, for example, will be slightly neutralized if contaminated with developer, but developer will be ruined by even a few drops of bleach.

Manufacturers always specify the temperatures at which their chemicals should be mixed – usually ranging from 68–104°F (20–40°C). You must achieve

these temperatures to be certain that complete mixing occurs. Sometimes, chemicals for a solution come in two or more parts, usually labeled A, B, C, and so on. Always mix these chemicals in the right order. Another rule is always add the chemicals to water, never the other way around. The equipment you need for processing are stirring rods (one for each chemical), funnels (one for each chemical), thermometer (thoroughly clean between uses), mixing beakers (one for each chemical), storage bottles, and waterproof gloves.

If they are kept away from extremes of temperature, chemical kits can be stored for a long time (check the use-by dates). Storage problems usually arise after chemicals have been mixed. To prevent oxidation and evaporation, store them in airtight containers filled to the brim. Concertina-type containers compress to exclude air before the cap is screwed tight.

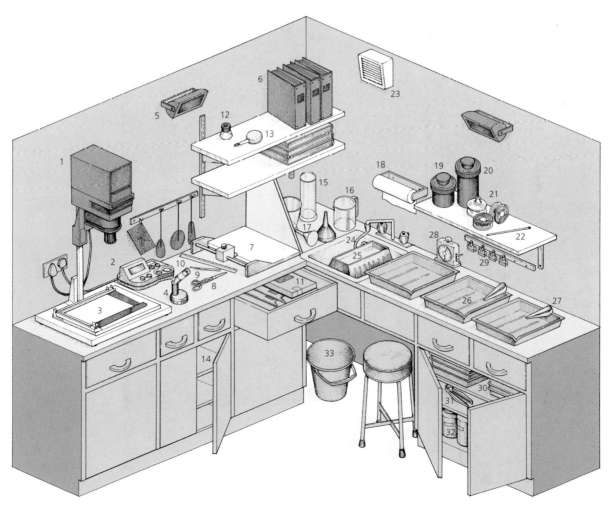

Dry area	5 Safelight	12 Magnifier	17 Funnels for pouring	22 Thermometer	28 Timer
1 Enlarger	6 Negative files	13 Blower brush	chemicals	23 Extractor fan	29 Rack for film clips
2 Combined exposure	7 Print trimmer	14 Storage area	18 Paper towels for	24 Rubber hose and	30 Spare print trays
timer and color	8 Scissors		mopping up spills	water filter	31 Film squeegee
analyzer	9 Scalpel	**Wet area**	19 Film developing tank	25 Print washer	tongs
3 Print easel	10 Ruler	15 Measuring cylinder	20 Color print drum	26 Print trays	32 Undiluted chemicals
4 Focus magnifier	11 Printing paper	16 Measuring jug	21 Film tank spirals	27 Print tongs	33 Bucket

Processing

Processing your own film adds hugely to the satisfaction of photography, giving you greater control over the quality of the work you produce. With a small darkroom you can process most films, color reversal (from which transparencies are produced) or color negatives. A few films, notably Kodachrome, can be processed only by specialist laboratories.

Read the instructions packed with your processing kit before you start and keep them handy for constant reference. Chemical choice depends on the type and make of film being developed, and you will get the best results by working within the time and temperature latitudes recommended by the makers.

LOADING THE FILM

Color film has to be removed from its cassette, loaded onto the film spiral, and placed in the developing tank in total darkness. Stainless-steel spirals and tanks are easier to keep clean than plastic ones, but many people find the plastic spirals easier to load. Because of the short developing times, it is essential that film is quickly and evenly covered in the chemical solution and quickly drained at the end of each stage.

When processing a single roll of film it is usual to place the loaded film spiral into the tank and then pour in the

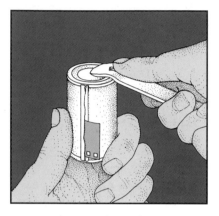

1 In total darkness, open the cassette using a bottle opener and remove the film. Avoid touching the film surface with your fingers.

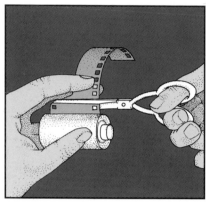

2 Cut the tapered film leader square with a pair of scissors, taking care to cut between the sprocket holes, since these help the film load onto the spiral.

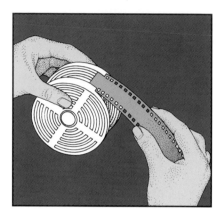

3 Wind the entire length of film onto the spiral and place it in the developing tank. Close the lid of the tank. You can now work in normal room light.

6 A few seconds before the end of the development time, quickly pour the developer back into a storage bottle through a filter and funnel.

7 Without opening the tank, pour in the next solution, also at the correct dilution and temperature. Start the timer.

8 At the end of the recommended processing time, quickly pour the chemical out of the tank into a storage bottle. Continue like this for all solutions.

PROCESSING SHEET FILM

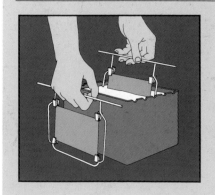

Sheet film 5 x 4in (12.7 x 10.2cm) and larger can be processed in deep tanks. Unload the film from its holder in total darkness and clip it by its corners onto stainless-steel hangers. Fit the hangers into the grooves on the tank so that the film is completely immersed in solution. Agitate by lifting the hanger from the tank and tilting it before replacing it in its grooves.

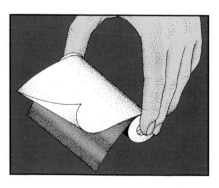

△ **Roll film,** such as 120 film, must be separated from its backing paper before you can load it onto a film spiral.

chemicals. The few seconds or so this takes will not affect development. Draining the tank, however, takes more time and this must count as part of the overall development period. When using a large tank to develop two or more rolls, however, pouring and draining take more time, so it is best to place the film in a tank into which chemicals have been poured. This ensures that the chemicals make contact evenly with the film.

DRIFT-BY TECHNIQUE

Once the film has been immersed, the tank needs to be agitated periodically to

4 Pour the developer through the opening in the light-tight tank. This solution must be at the correct dilution and temperature. Start the timer.

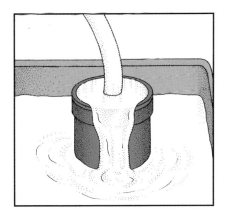

9 Complete the fixing process according to the maker's instructions and then wash the film in running water for at least 30 minutes.

make sure the chemicals are evenly distributed. With small, light-tight tanks, all you need do is invert the tank – rapping the tank on the edge of the bench dislodges any air bubbles adhering to the film surface, which would prevent chemicals reaching the emulsion beneath. Large tanks have a rod that threads through the middle of the spirals, and you agitate the chemicals by raising and lowering the rod.

Developing temperatures are critical. In less than ideal conditions, it is difficult to keep the temperature of any solution constant throughout the period it is in

5 Lightly rap the tank on the edge of the bench to dislodge air bubbles. During development, invert the tank as recommended in the maker's instructions.

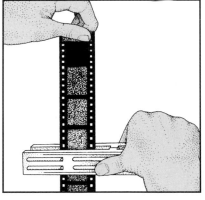

10 Drain the water and unwind the film from the spiral. Remove excess water with squeegee tongs and hang the film to dry in a dust-free area.

the tank. To overcome this problem you can use the "drift-by" technique, which involves raising the temperature of the developer to its upper limit just before it is used and then allowing it to drop toward the lower limit during the period it is in the tank. Say, for example, the manufacturer recommends a latitude of 0.5° above and below a specified temperature. In effect, this means you have a 1° safety margin through which the temperature of the chemicals can drift between the time you pour them in at the upper temperature limit and the time you pour them out.

Some modern chemistry kits that are designed specifically for home darkroom use provide a range of temperatures at which film can be developed. Processing at lower temperatures is accomplished by extending the development time. Temperature control, however, is just as important as it is for processes that are carried out at higher temperatures.

DRYING AND STORING

Wet film has a milky, opaque look that disappears as it dries. Immediately after removing the film from its final wash, clean it down with a squeegee to make sure it dries evenly and without any water spots. Then hang the film in a warm, dust-free area or, better still, in a thermostatically controlled drying cabinet.

Take care to avoid splashing partially dry film with water. If the film does get splashed, quickly place the whole roll in water, wash it briefly, and dry it again.

To avoid damaging the emulsion and to stop the film curling excessively, the drying temperature should not not exceed 100°F (38°C). When it is dry, cut the film up into strips for negatives and store them in moisture-proof, acid-free sleeves. If reversal film, carefully cut the film up into single frames and mount those not intended for printing.

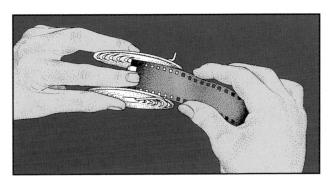

△ **Stainless-steel spirals** are loaded from the center of the spiral. A clip holds the cut end of the film in place and then you rotate the spiral as the film falls into the grooves. If the film jams, unwind enough to free it and try again. Don't force it.

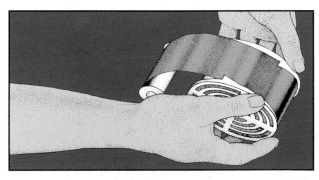

△ **Plastic spirals** are loaded from the outside. Slip the cut end of the film under the film guides and twist each side of the spiral alternately to draw the film in. The spiral must be completely dry or the film may stick to the grooves.

Printing from negatives

The first stage in the process of printing from negatives is to make a set of contact sheets showing small images of everything on your roll of film. Not only is this the least expensive way of previewing your pictures, it also provides you with a positive record of your negatives.

Begin by exposing and processing a test strip of the contacts, initially using the filtration recommended by the paper manufacturer and altering the exposures in steps of 15, 30, and 45 seconds. Then, adjusting the filtration and exposure according to the results of the test strip, produce a final full set of contacts. Since they are only an intermediate stage, the contacts need not be exact for color or density as you will be able to make further corrections on the test strips of the negatives you later decide to print.

It is vital to keep a detailed record of exposure and filtration details, beginning with the very first test strip of the contacts and following through to the assessments and adjustments made at each stage of making the final print. You will then have all the relevant data should you wish to make a reprint. Color analyzers assess the light transmitted through the negative and make recommendations regarding filtration. These can save you a lot of time making test strips and the cost of paper and processing chemicals. However, still make a note of all relevant settings in case you want to make adjustments or produce a non-standard-looking print.

Printing equipment
An optional piece of printing equipment is a color analyzer, which can save you time in the darkroom and minimize wasted materials.

1 Crank for adjusting height of enlarger head
2 Enlarger column
3 Enlarger color head with dial-in filters
4 Exposure timer
5 Processing timer
6 Enlarger baseboard
7 Print easel
8 Measuring jug
9 Warming bath for processing chemicals
10 Scissors
11 Thermometer
12 Gloves
13 Measuring cylinders
14 Print processing drum

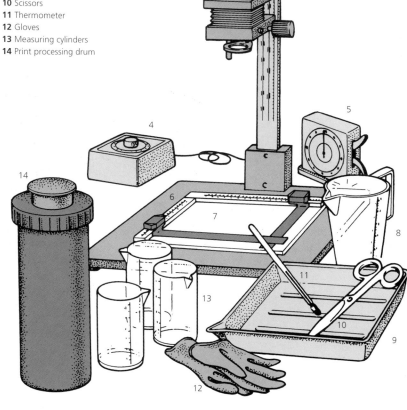

CORRECTING COLOR

When you have processed and dried the first test strip, find one of the bands that appears to be about correct in terms of exposure. Examine the color in that part. Color is best assessed by comparison, so make sure that a portion of the test strip includes a color that can readily be checked, such as a flesh tone against your own hand.

Color casts can be removed by increasing or decreasing the yellow (Y), magenta (M), and cyan (C) filtration controls on your enlarger's color head. The initial recommended filtration provides a starting point when making your first test strip, but this is only a rough guide. Due to a number of factors – including lighting quality in the original photograph, the age of the film or paper,

variations in the temperature of processing chemicals – some degree of correction is always needed. One way of assessing this is by viewing the test strip through special filters. But bear in mind that the photographic effect is greater than the visual one, so adjust enlarger filtration by only half the amount indicated by the viewing filters.

Additions to filtration will reduce the amount of light passing through the enlarger's lens; decreases will let more light through. Details of exposure adjustments for specific filters are given in the enlarger's instructions.

PRINTING PAPER

Although printing paper for color work does not come in different contrast grades, you do have a choice of surface.

A glossy finish helps to produce specular highlights in shots of water or jewelry, while many people choose a semi-matt surface for printing portraits or landscape shots. Textured surfaces, such as stipple or silk, are less visually brilliant but involve no loss of color quality.

All color papers are coated first with a synthetic resin, then with a light-sensitive emulsion layer. The emulsion is very susceptible to the acid in your fingerprints, so handle the paper by its edges or wear clean cotton gloves. Special print dryers can dry resin-coated paper in a matter of minutes, but an ordinary hair dryer can do the job just as well. Improper storage causes changes in the color balance and speed of paper. To minimize these changes, ideally keep unexposed paper refrigerated.

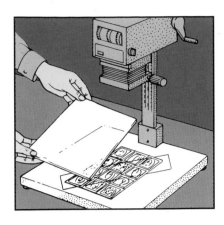

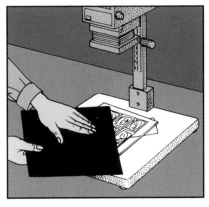

1 Before making a full set of contacts, you first have to print a test strip to assess exposure times and filtration. A methodical approach to the color darkroom is essential, so use a notebook to keep records of all exposures and filtration settings. Dial in recommended filtration and then, in darkness, place a strip of paper across the baseboard. Lay the negatives emulsion side down on the paper and cover the negatives with a sheet of clean glass.

2 Hold the glass near the edges to avoid leaving fingerprints over the area covered by the printing paper. Place a piece of black card over two-thirds of the test strip and expose for 15 seconds. Move the card down one-third and give another 15 seconds exposure. Finally, remove the card and give the whole strip another 15 seconds. The final third of the strip will have received 15 seconds, the middle third 30 seconds, and the first third 45 seconds.

3 Place the strip of printing paper inside a print drum (emulsion side inward). Once the lid of the drum is in place, you can process the strip in normal room lighting. Following the dilution and temperature recommendations of your chemical chosen processing kit, pour each solution into and out of the light-trapped opening in the top of the drum. Replace the cap and roll the drum on the surface of the bench to distribute the chemicals evenly.

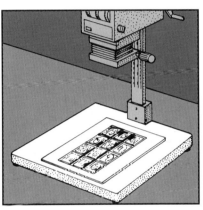

4 Remove the test strip from the drum, handling the paper by one edge only. When the emulsion is wet, it is very vulnerable to damage. Air-dry the print in a warm, dust-free area or use a hair dryer to speed the process up. Once dry, find an area that seems closest to the correct exposure and assess the color there. In the notebook used to record settings, strike out previous exposure and filtration notations and note down necessary adjustments.

5 Dial in revised filtration and set the timer to the new exposure. In darkness, lay the negatives down on a full sheet of paper and cover them again with a sheet of clean glass. Turn on the enlarger and expose. Process and dry the contact sheet. If you are satisfied with the results, file the contact sheets with your record notes, filling in any adjustments needed to correct the exposure and filtration.

CORRECTING FILTRATION

If the color cast displayed on your test strip is only slight, adjust the filtration by ±5 to 10 units of density. If the color cast is moderate, adjust filtration by ±20 units. If the cast is considerable, try ±30 units of density. You can, of course, dial in intermediate densities of filtration for fine tuning color corrections. Bear in mind that if the yellow, magenta, and cyan filters are all in use, the amount they overlap equals neutral density. This will increase overall exposure time, and so you always want one set of filters set to 0.

Color cast	Filter settings
Yellow	+Y or -M and C
Magenta	+M or -Y and C
Cyan	+C or -Y and M
Red	+Y and M or -C
Green	+Y and C or -M
Blue	+M and C or -Y

TEST STRIP FOR ENLARGEMENTS

Before printing an enlargement, you need to make another test strip. Your contact sheet is at best a compromise, since it has to take in the exposure and filtration requirements of many different images. The size of the enlargement depends on the quality of the negative and the enlarger lens, the maximum height of the enlarger column, and the degree of acceptable graininess. Pearl-, stipple-, or silk-finish papers, because of their textured surface, help to disguise graininess. As a rough guide only, the largest print from a 35mm negative is 10 x 12in (25 x 30cm), and from a 2¼ x 2¼in (6 x 6cm) negative, 16 x 20in (40 x 50cm).

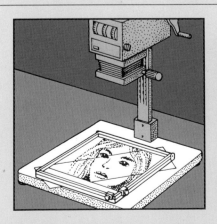

1 Dial in filtration based on your last assessment. Place a negative in the carrier, emulsion side down. Compose the enlarged image on the baseboard. Turn the enlarger off and, in darkness, place a test strip in position. Expose the paper.

2 Process and dry the test strip. Once it is dry, check it against a neutral background (a strongly colored background will influence your assessment). If there is a color cast, determine correction needed by examining the strip through viewing filters.

Printing from transparencies

Paper and chemical manufacturers are constantly making improvements in their products, simplifying processing steps and increasing the range of working temperatures within which accurate prints can be achieved, and now the home darkroom worker can produce exhibition-quality prints directly from transparencies. Although most photographers still consider that color negatives produce the finest-quality prints, others think this is offset by the distinct advantages of shooting with reversal, or transparency, film.

For one thing, processed transparency film gives positive images that are immediately ready for viewing after the film processing stage. There is no difficulty in telling whether or not the colors in the transparency are accurate, something that is next to impossible to do when viewing color negatives, in which colors and tones are reversed and an overall color mask distorts what colors can be seen. Even more important – for professional photographers, at least – is that magazine and book picture editors prefer to use transparencies for reproduction in their publications.

CHOOSING A TRANSPARENCY
You do need to bear in mind that the photographic papers used in positive-positive printing (in other words, making a positive print from a positive original) are inherently contrasty, and so results will likely be better if the contrast in the original transparency is not too extreme.

The ideal transparency for positive-positive printing is one that is slightly underexposed – that is, one in which there is greater than normal color saturation. But, however perfect the transparency, exposure times and filtration will still have to be determined through a process of trial and error. This is because different types of film vary in their color characteristics and, similarly, enlargers vary in the nature of their light output.

Once you are satisfied that a print you have produced matches the original transparency for both color and density, you do need to vary exposure and

1 Select a transparency (unmount it if necessary) and place it in the carrier of the enlarger emulsion side down. Handle the film carefully – tiny flecks of dust are enlarged along with the image and reproduce as black spots. Compose and focus the image and, with room and enlarger lights off, position the test strip, emulsion side up, on the part of the easel where the image showed the most representative tones.

2 Cover two-thirds of the test strip with a piece of card and expose. After 15 seconds, move the card to reveal another third of the strip. After a further 15 seconds, remove the card to expose the complete strip. This gives three expose bands: 15, 30, and 45 seconds. Remove the strip from the easel and load it into the processing drum, still in complete darkness. Carefully curl the paper with the emulsion side inward.

3 Once the lid of the processing drum is in place, you can turn the room lights on. Check the temperature of your first processing solution and, if it is within the recommended tolerances, pour it into the the light-trapped opening in the lid. It is best to wear waterproof gloves when handling any chemicals. As soon as you have finished pouring in the solution, start the timer.

4 To ensure that all of the emulsion area of the test strip is evenly coated in developer solution, place the cap firmly on the drum, turn it on its side, and roll it back and forth continuously on a flat surface, such as the top of the darkroom work bench, throughout the development stage.

5 Return the developer solution to a proper storage container. Use a funnel with a built-in filter to preserve as much of the liquid as possible. Always note the number and size of prints processed to gauge exhaustion. Consider the length of time it takes to drain the print drum – anywhere from about 5 to 15 seconds depending on design and capacity – as part of the total development time.

6 If necessary, wash the print between chemical processes with clean water at the recommended temperature. Then repeat the previous steps for each chemical solution in your kit. After processing is complete, carefully remove the strip from the drum, taking care not to damage the still fragile emulsion. Air dry the print in a warm, dust-free area before assessing color and filtration.

filtration settings for subsequent prints made from the same batch of paper. If, however, you want multiple prints to be identical in color and density, you need to keep tight control over all the print-processing steps.

PAPER TYPES

There are two different systems of paper suitable for making prints from transparencies, and the manufacturers of each provide processing materials and chemicals for use at home in an averagely equipped darkroom. As well as these, independent processing kits are available.

Although the two systems may look superficially similar, it is important to note that they are not interchangeable. One is a "chromogenic" system, in which colors are created in the printing material by chemical reaction with the developer. In the other system, known as "dye-destruction", colorfast dyes are incorporated into different layers of the emulsion of the printing material, and these are revealed by the destruction of the layers above. Whatever system you use, always read and follow the manufacturer's instructions.

WORKING PRACTICES

Because of the broad color sensitivity of the materials, color darkroom workers have to discipline themselves to working in total darkness, or under safelighting that is so dim as to be of little use. This applies to the exposure of the paper until it is safely inside the print-processing drum. It is always best to do positive-positive printing in volume to make best use of the chemicals, so on average aim to complete six to ten prints from the same number of transparencies during a three-hour session in the darkroom.

Obviously, this will depend, among other things, on the capacity of your equipment, but experience and a methodical approach will increase the number of prints you can complete in any given time.

EXPOSURE

Unless you are using an exposure meter and a color analyzer, you need to establish the correct exposure and filtration manually by making a test print. To do this, in total darkness cut a strip off a sheet of printing paper, about one-third of its width. Remember to replace all printing paper back in its light-tight bag before turning on room

lights again. As a starting point, it is a good idea to use the suggested settings regarding exposure and filtration that accompany all processing kits. Adjust the enlarger controls accordingly and compose the image from the transparency on the enlarger easel, moving the head up and down on its column until you achieve the correct degree of enlargement. It is a good idea to check the focus of the image at full aperture, since this gives the brightest projected image, and then close the lens aperture down to its working aperture.

Then, with the room lights and enlarger off, lay the test strip across the easel and expose it section by section at 15-second intervals. The first part of the test strip will, thus, receive 45 seconds exposure, the middle part 30 seconds, and the final part only 15 seconds. After processing the strip, you need to assess density and color before progressing.

When assessing color, compare the test strip results with the original transparency under good viewing conditions – daylight is preferable. Decide which of the three exposures is correct and check the colors critically in that area. Bear in mind that color will appear darker when the print is wet. Note also that the effects of exposure and filtration are opposite to those in printing negatives, whether black and white or color. If, for example, the print is too light, it has been overexposed rather than underexposed (see the box on the right for guidance on correcting density and color).

DRUM PROCESSING

Many types of rotary drum processors are available. All are tubular containers with light-tight lids, designed to use a minimum of processing solution. The amount of liquid needed will vary according to the volume of the drum and the size of the printing paper being processed. Precise information is included in the manufacturer's instructions.

Always take care to to remain within the recommended tolerances of time and temperature, and if you do vary the standard processing in any way, make a careful note so you can reproduce results at some later time. Mix the chemicals in clean measuring cylinders and bring them up to the recommended temperature. Any tools, such as mixing rods that are used in more than one solution, must be cleaned thoroughly

after being in contact with any chemical to avoid contamination. You can maintain the temperature of solutions throughout the darkroom session by standing the cylinders in a shallow tray of warm water, the temperature of which you will need to monitor constantly, topping up with hot water as necessary.

Because you handle all color printing materials in darkness, or under very dime safelighting, it is essential to have all necessary equipment close at hand so that you locate it quickly and safely after the print has been exposed and during the processing stages. The illustrations opposite show a representative processing sequence concentrating on good darkroom practice. The actual number of stages varies from kit to kit.

DENSITY AND COLOR

CORRECTING DENSITY
Print is very dark: Open the aperture of the enlarger lens by one full f stop.
Print is slightly dark: Open the aperture of the enlarger lens by ½ an f stop.
Print is slightly light: Close the aperture of the enlarger lens by ½ an f stop.
Print is very light: Close the aperture of the enlarger lens by one full f stop.

CORRECTING COLOR BALANCE
Yellow color cast is evident: Decrease filtration by 20Y, using the dial-in control on color head.
Magenta color cast is evident: Decrease filtration by 20M, using the dial-in control on color head.
Cyan color cast is evident: Decrease filtration by 20C, using the dial-in control on color head.
Blue color cast is evident: Decrease filtration by 20M + 20C, using the dial-in controls on color head.
Green color cast is evident: Decrease filtration by 20Y + 20C, using the dial-in controls on color head.
Red color cast is evident: Decrease filtration by 20Y + 20M, using the dial-in controls on color head.

Identifying and correcting faults

△ **Fault:** Subject blurred and oddly angled.
Cause: Subject too close coupled with careless camera handling.
Remedy: Check carefully on the focusing screen of an SLR that the subject is sharply focused before shooting. You will find the minimum focusing distance for a particular lens on the focusing scale on the barrel (or in your camera's user's manual), and all important subject elements should be positioned at least that distance away. With a compact camera, the viewfinder does not show the actual image formed by the lens and so you must pay careful attention to minimum focusing distance. Unless you intentionally want oddly angled framing, try to align the top or side of the viewfinder image with a horizontal or vertical line somewhere within the image area.

Fault: Part or all of the image is soft or indistinct.
Cause: Dirty or dusty lens or lens filter.
Remedy: Dirt, greasy finger marks, or dust on the front element of the lens or on a lens filter will cause light entering the lens to scatter slightly, reducing its image-resolving power. Carefully clean the lens, following the manufacturer's recommendations, and then keep a clear-glass or UV or skylight filter over the lens at all times to protect it. Clean the filter regularly, and if it becomes scratched it can be replaced at minimal cost.

△ **Fault:** All of image is blurred.
Cause: Camera shake.
Remedy: Use a faster shutter speed or support the camera on a firm surface or tripod if this is not possible. If you are using aperture-priority exposure control, selecting a wider aperture will force the camera to select a faster shutter speed to compensate. Adopting the right stance while taking a picture can minimize camera shake: stand with your feet comfortably apart; support the camera with both hands; make sure your shoulders are relaxed; breathe in and hold as you take the picture; and press the shutter release gently – don't jab downward.

Fault: Subject is blurred while static parts of the scene are sharp.
Cause: Subject movement.
Remedy: Use a faster shutter speed with moving subjects. Bear in mind that subjects traveling at 90° to the camera require the fastest shutter speed to "freeze" movement; those traveling at the same speed but at 45° to the camera can be "frozen" using a slower shutter speed; and subjects traveling either directly toward or away from the camera can be "frozen" using the slowest shutter speed of all.

△ **Fault:** Area of non-image-forming flare.
Cause: Including the sun, or other bright light sources, in the picture area.
Remedy: Exclude the sun, or other light source, from the image and check the viewfinder for evidence of flare affecting the image from outside the picture area. Attaching a screw-on lens hood will prevent flare coming in from the sides of the frame, or you can shade the front of the lens with your hand. If all else fails, change your camera position so that some feature in the scene, such as tree foliage, obscures the light source.

△ **Fault:** Irregular blotches of color, or low-contrast image.
Cause: Incorrect processing, such as uneven development or fogging.
Remedy: Make sure that air bubbles do not form on the surface of the film during processing, since this will prevent chemicals reaching the surface of the emulsion. Rapping the developing tank on the edge of the workbench is usually sufficient to dislodge air bubbles. This should be followed by regular agitation, as recommended. One type of fogging is caused by white light reaching the film before it is properly fixed. Check that the top of the tank is firmly in place and that you load the film into the tank in complete darkness.

△ **Fault:** Film physically damaged and holed.
Cause: Trying to squeeze too many frames out of a roll of film.
Remedy: With manual film-loading cameras you normally have to wind the first three frames on (after closing the camera back) before starting to take pictures. This allows sufficient waste film at the beginning of a roll for film to overcome fogging and to allow processors to attach film-handling clips. If you only wind on the first one or two frames, your first image may be physically damaged during processing. Most cameras now feature automatic film transport, which winds sufficient film on at the beginning to overcome this potential problem. Film manufacturers allow for three frames of waste, so you will still not be cheated out of any pictures.

△ **Fault:** Final frame incomplete.
Cause: End of roll encountered.
Remedy: Check the camera's frame counter to make sure that on, say, a 24- or 36-exposure roll of film you take only 24 or 36 exposures, even if the film appears to wind on after the final picture is taken. You may be able to squeeze an extra frame or two out of a roll, but you take a risk that one of those pictures may be spoiled.

△ **Fault:** Unexpected overall color cast.
Cause: Using a filter intended for black and white film with color film.
Remedy: Lens filters designed for use with black and white film often have a distinct overall color, the purpose of which is to alter the tonal response of the film to specific colors of light. For example, a yellow filter will help to increase the contrast between sky and clouds by causing the film to register blue as a slightly darker tone. If, however, you change from black and white to color film and neglect to remove the filter, all resulting pictures will have a cast corresponding to the color of the filter.

△ **Fault:** Pupils of subject's eyes bright red.
Cause: Flash too close to camera lens.
Remedy: This problem occurs when the flash and the lens are on almost the same axis and the camera records light reflecting back from the veins behind the pupils of the subject's eyes. With detachable accessory flash, use an extension lead to distance camera and flash, or angle the flash head so that its light is reflected from a wall or the ceiling before reaching the subject. Cameras (predominantly compacts) with built-in, front-facing flash often have a "red-eye-reduction" feature. This consists of two or three pre-flashes, designed to cause the subject's pupils to contract, before the main flash fires.

△ **Fault:** Negatives that are too dense or slides that are too thin.
Cause: Overexposure.
Remedy: Overexposure occurs when too much light reaches the film, and there could be numerous causes for this problem. First, check that you have set the correct film speed on the camera – changing to a faster film without recalibrating the meter will result in overexposure. On DX-coded cameras, the film-speed-recognition sensors may be faulty and need repairing. Second, the mechanisms controlling the shutter speed or aperture may not be working properly and need repairing. Finally, the sensors in the camera that register the amount of light reaching the film may not be working properly. If only an occasional frame of film is overexposed, you may not be aware of how your exposure meter is designed to work and are allowing it to be over-influenced by an unrepresentatively dark part of the scene. This will cause the camera to set a shutter speed/aperture combination that overexposes the majority of a frame of film. Check your user's manual for further information about your meter.

△ **Fault:** Overall blue color cast.
Cause: Using film designed to be exposed under tungsten light in daylight or electronic flash.
Remedy: Use a special orange-colored filter over the camera lens to produce the correct color balance. Always check that you are using the appropriate film for the dominant light source.

Fault: Overall orange color cast
Cause: Using film designed to be exposed under daylight conditions in tungsten light, such as indoor domestic lighting
Remedy: Use a special blue-colored filter over the camera lens to produce the correct color balance. Always check that you are using the appropriate film for the dominant light source.

△ **Fault:** Images superimposed (double exposure).
Cause: Faulty film advance leading to two (or more) images appearing on the same frame. This can also occur if you put a previously exposed film back into the camera.
Remedy: If a film is not loaded properly, it may slip and not wind-on as it should after each exposure. If this is not the case, then the camera will need to be repaired to eliminate the problem. Double exposure can also occur if a previously exposed (but unprocessed) film is loaded into the camera and re-exposed. If you wind the film leader back into the cassette after finishing a roll, this cannot happen. APS cassettes cannot be accidentally double exposed.

△ **Fault:** Negatives that are too thin or slides that are too dense.
Cause: Underexposure.
Remedy: Underexposure occurs when too little light reaches the film, and there could be numerous causes for this problem (see Overexposure), such as changing to slower film without changing the film-speed setting on the camera. If only an occasional frame of film is underexposed, you may not be aware of how your exposure meter is designed to work and are allowing it to be over-influenced by an unrepresentatively bright part of the scene. This will cause the camera to set a shutter speed/aperture combination that underexposes the majority of a frame of film. Check your user's manual for further information about your meter.

Glossary

Aberration General term for image faults caused by an imperfect lens. *See also* Astigmatism, Barrel and Pincushion distortion, Chromatic aberration, Coma, Spherical aberration.

Absorption Taking up of light energy by matter and its transformation into heat. Surfaces that are seen as colored usually absorb some of the components of the light falling on them and reflect others. For example, a red surface absorbs green and blue light, reflecting red light.

Achromatic Describes colors that contain equal mixtures of the three primary colors of light and so display no hue but vary only in lightness. These range through the grays from white to black.

Achromatic lens Lens that brings two colors of the spectrum, usually blue and green, to the same point of focus.

Acid fixer Stabilizing solution containing a weak acid that neutralizes any residual developer in the final stages of processing.

Actinic Describes the ability of light to produce changes in materials exposed to it – in photographic emulsions, for example. Blue light is especially actinic.

Acutance Scientific term for the sharpness with which a photographic material can record images at various levels of contrast.

Additive color process A means of producing a color image by mix blue, green, and red colored lights in proportions corresponding to those reflected by the original subject.

Additive primaries Blue, green, and red lights of a saturated hue, which, when mixed together in varying combinations or intensities can give any other color.

Aerial perspective Effect of depth created by haze in a photograph. Distant objects are recorded with lighter tones and with colors distorted toward blue, giving a three-dimensional impression.

After image Persistence of an image after the original stimulus to the retina of the eye has ceased. Because of fatigue to the cones (color receptors), the colors of the after image may be complementary to those initially registered.

Agitation Movement set up between photographic material and processing solutions to ensure uniform action of the solutions.

Air-bells Bubbles of air clinging to the emulsion surface during processing and, thus, preventing chemical action.

Angle of view The angle formed between the lens and the most widely separated points on a distant subject that the lens can form a sharp image of on the film format. Usually the diagonal from opposite corners of the film is taken as the base.

Anti-halation backing Coating of dye or pigment to prevent the reflection of light from the near surface of the film support.

Aperture Area, usually variable, of lens through which light enters the camera, the size of which is controlled by the diaphragm.

ASA film speed Arithmetical system of rating the emulsion speed of photographic materials laid down by the American Standards Association. This system is now no longer used – *see* ISO.

Astigmatism Off-axis aberration causing vertical and horizontal lines to be focused in different focal planes.

Backlighting Lighting from behind the subject. Often produces a fringing, or halo, of light separating subject from background.

Ball-and-socket head Mounting on the top of a tripod that permits the camera to pivot in any direction by the loosening of one control.

Barn doors Hinged flaps surrounding a lighting head to control the spread of light.

Barrel distortion Distortion of the image where straight lines at the edge of the field of view of the lens bend inward at the corners of the frame.

Batch numbers Serial numbers marked by manufacturers on each batch of photographic film or paper. Can be invaluable in tracing and proving faults of manufacture. For consistency, photographers order film or paper with the same batch numbers.

Bellows Light-tight folding sleeve between camera body and lens. A bellows focusing unit can be used to provide additional extension between lens and body when taking close-ups.

Between-the-lens shutter Shutter with light-obscuring blades that is placed between the lens elements close to the diaphragm. Also known as an interlens shutter.

Bleaching Process of converting metallic silver into an almost colorless compound such as a silver halide, which can then be reduced, dissolved, or dyed.

Bloom Transparent coating on a lens glass to suppress reflections. *See* Coated lens.

Bounced flash Flash illumination reflected from a surface, such as a wall or ceiling, before reaching the subject, thus being diffused.

Bracketing Taking extra shots of a subject, doubling and halving the exposure judged to be correct. Prudent where a shot is important and there is an uneven balance of light.

Brightness range The difference in brightness between the lightest and darkest areas of a scene or image.

B setting Mark on the shutter speed dial indicating that the shutter will open when the release button is depressed and stay open until pressure is released.

Burning in Extra exposure given to particular areas of a print as a means of selective darkening.

Cable release A wire moving within an outer sheath allowing the camera shutter to be triggered from a distance and, thus, reducing vibration.

Camera movements Means of altering the relative planes of a camera back and lens panel. Also of moving the lens at right angles to its axis. Movements are generally found only on large cameras, but lenses with rise and fall are made for the 35mm SLR camera format.

Cassette A light-tight container for 35mm film. In the camera, film is wound back into the cassette after exposure.

Cast Overall shift of colors in an image toward a particular part of the spectrum, often due to a disparity between the color temperature of a light source and the color balance of the film.

Catadioptric lens Lens utilizing a mirror and reducing the overall lens dimensions in extreme long-focus design.

Chromatic aberration Image fault caused by the inability of a lens to bring light of all colors to a common point of focus.

Circle of confusion An image disk produced by a lens from a point source of light. The smaller the disk the sharper the image.

Close-up lens Auxiliary lens used in conjunction with a normal lens for close focusing.

Coated lens Lens with surfaces coated with thin layers of a hard substance, such as magnesium fluoride, to minimize light loss or fogging caused by reflections from the lens. The thickness of the coating is a precise fraction of an average wavelength of light, so that reflection from the coating material is intermediate between that of air and glass.

Color analyzer Device for measuring the color of a projected color image in order to make corrections with color filters when printing.

Color blindness Inability to distinguish between different hues. Most commonly, the defect is partial –

a failure to discriminate certain pairs of colors because either red- or green-sensitive cones in the retina of the eye do not function normally.

Color negative film Film that records the colors of the subject in complementary hues that are subsequently reversed again in the printing paper to give correct colors.

Color reversal film Film that produces a direct positive image by effectively "reversing" the negative image during processing. In transparency film, which is of this type, color dyes are produced in image areas wherever a layer of the tripack emulsion did not record light from the subject. By subtracting colors from the white light in which they are viewed, these dyes reproduce the original colors of the subject.

Color temperature The measurement of a light source in terms of the energy distribution over the spectrum and, hence, the color quality. Theoretically related to the appearance of a heated "black body", it is expressed in degrees kelvin.

Coma An off-axis lens aberration resulting in a point of light being reproduced as a disk with a comet-like tail.

Complementary colors Any two colors that, when mixed, will produce an achromatic color, white, gray, or black. The complementary color pairs used in most color film and printing processes are red-cyan, green-magenta, and clue-yellow.

Cones Tiny cone-shaped organs in the retina containing pigments that absorb certain wavelengths of light. Signals from these light receptors, analyzed in the nervous system, lead to the sensation of different colors. The cones are of three main classes, responding most strongly to either blue, green, or red light.

Contrast Difference between the light and dark tones in a subject or image, and also between colors that lie opposite each other on the color wheel.

Converging lens Lens that is thicker in the middle than at the edges, making parallel rays of light converge to a point of focus. All camera lenses are converging overall.

Converging verticals Effect produced when the camera is pointed away from a parallel position. Vertical lines, such as the sides of buildings, appear to lean in toward the top of the photograph.

Converter Auxiliary lens used in conjunction with a camera lens to produce a lens system of different focal length.

Correction filter General term for filters used to alter colors to suit the color response of the film.

Coupled rangefinder Device that focuses the camera lens as the rangefinder is adjusted to the correct distance by making two images of the subject coincide when seen in the viewfinder.

Covering power The maximum size of film on which the lens will produce an image of acceptable quality.

Curvature of field Lens aberration that causes the image to be focused on a curved plane instead of a flat surface.

Cut film Large-format film supplied in flat sheets for individual exposures.

Daylight film Reversal film balanced for use in average daylight illumination or electronic flash of about 5,500K.

Definition Sharpness of the image produced by a lens or recorded by a film.

Delayed action Operation of a camera mechanism that produces a delay between depressing the shutter release and the exposure being made. Used to reduce vibration and to enable the photographer to be included in the picture.

Depth of field The distance over which objects remain acceptably sharp both behind and in front of the point on which the lens is focused. Within this zone, the distance behind the plane of focus is usually twice as great as the distance in front of it. This does not hold true with close subjects.

Depth of focus Focusing latitude – the distance through which the film can be moved, parallel to the optical axis, after the lens has been focused while still producing an acceptably sharp image.

Developer Chemical bath that produces a visible image of metallic silver, sometimes with associated dyes, from the latent image formed on film or print emulsion by light.

Diaphragm Adjustable aperture of a lens, usually controlled by a set of curved metallic blades that opens and closes around a central opening.

Diffraction Scattering of light rays around the edge of an opaque substance, particularly noticeable when light passes through a small hole. Diffraction softens the edge of shadows, as some light bends around the edge.

Diffusion Scattering of light passing through a translucent but not transparent medium such as tracing paper or a smoky atmosphere. Diffused light is softer and lower in contrast.

Dodging Term for shading when exposing a print on the enlarger baseboard to produce a lighter result.

Double exposure Result of exposing a film twice. With many cameras the film advance and shutter setting are interlocked to prevent accidental double exposure. Automatic film advance also makes double exposure impossible.

Drift-by technique Means of using the latitude available in maintaining the temperature of processing solutions, by starting a few degrees above the correct temperature and finishing a few degrees below it.

Drying marks Blemishes left by the evaporation of droplets of water on the film or print surface.

Dry mounting Method of fixing prints onto mounts by using heat-sensitive adhesive, usually in the form of a tissue.

Electronic flash Lighting unit utilizing the pulse of light produced by discharging a current between two electrodes in a gas-filled tube.

Emulsion General term for the light-sensitive layer, consisting of silver halides in gelatin, used in the production of films and printing papers.

Enlargement Print larger than the original negative or transparency.

Expiration date Manufacturer's indication of the working life of a sensitized material. As films age the fog level rises, speed falls, and the color balance begins to alter.

Exposure counter Mechanical or electronic device on a camera showing the number of film exposures already taken.

Exposure latitude Range over which exposure can be varied and still produce an acceptable result.

Exposure meter Device for measuring the light falling on or reflected from the subject. Usually the measurement is expressed in terms of shutter speeds and aperture sizes.

Extension tubes Tubes that can be attached in various combinations between the lens and camera body to facilitate a range of close-focusing distances.

Fast lens A lens that has a wide aperture in relation to its focal length – for example, a 50mm lens with, say, a maximum aperture of f1.2, or a 400mm telephoto lens with a maximum aperture of f4.5.

Fill-in Light directed on a subject to illuminate shadows cast by the principal light source.

Film plane Plane on which film is positioned inside the camera. Coincides with the focus plane.

Film speed Means of representing numerically the response of a photographic material to light.

Filter Material that absorbs certain portions of light and transmits the remainder. Color filters absorb selected wavelengths while neutral density filters absorb equal portions of all visible wavelengths.

Fish-eye lens Extreme wide-angle lens covering an angle of about 180° to 220° and producing a distorted image with central objects at a larger scale than those toward the edges.

Fixed-focus lens A permanently focused lens usually permitting acceptably sharp pictures to be taken beyond about 5ft (1.5m).

Fixing Stabilizing an image by removing excess silver halide or converting it to a soluble complex.

Flare Scattered light produced by reflections inside the lens and camera. Flare reduces image contrast.

F number Numerical expression of the light passing power of a lens at its different stop settings. Equal to the focal length of the lens divided by its effective aperture.

Focal length In the case of a simple lens, the distance between the lens and the position of a sharply focused image on the film plane when the lens is focused at infinity.

Focal plane Plane on which a lens forms a sharp image when correctly focused.

Focal plane shutter Type of shutter where the blinds or blades are placed behind the lens, as near to the focal plane as possible.

Focusing The adjustment of the lens-to-film distance to produce a sharp image of the subject. Closer subjects require greater lens-to-film distance.

Focusing screen Etched glass or plastic used in a camera as an aid to observing and focusing the image before exposure.

Gelatin Colloid of animal origin used as the binding medium for silver halides in photographic emulsions.

Graininess Visual impression of the irregularly distributed clumps of silver grains or their associated dye images, which form the photographic image.

Granularity Scientific assessment of grain as opposed to the subjective impression that is termed graininess.

Ground-glass screen Translucent screen used for viewing and focusing in large-format and reflex camera formats.

Guide number An indication of the power of a flash unit, enabling the correct aperture to be selected at a given distance between flash and subject. The guide number divided by the distance gives the f stop that should be used. A film speed is specified with the guide number, and so recalculation is needed for films of different speeds.

Halation Diffused secondary image caused by light reflected back up through the emulsion from the film support.

Halogen Generic term for elements in the iodine, bromine, chlorine, and fluorine groups. Compounds of metals with these elements are called halides. Light-sensitive silver halides form the basis of photographic film and paper emulsions.

Hardener Chemical used to increase the mechanical toughness of gelatin and raise its melting point.

High key Describes an image that consists mainly of light, delicate tones. This type of imagery may be helped by slight overexposure.

Highlights Bright parts of the subject, which reproduce as the densest areas in the negative and as the lightest areas in prints or transparencies.

Hot shoe Accessory shoe, usually located on top of a camera, with a contact for flash synchronization that match another contact on the foot of the flashgun.

Hue The quality that distinguishes one color from another and that changes when a surface reflects a different mixture of spectral light.

Hyperfocal distance Distance from the lens to the nearest point that is acceptably sharp when the lens is focused at infinity. By refocusing on this point the depth of field can be extended in front of it by half the hyperfocal distance. Fixed-focus lenses are often set to the hyperfocal distance.

Hypo Popular name for sodium thiosulfate, once the universal fixing agent for dissolving unwanted silver halides in photographic emulsions. A hypo eliminator is an oxidizing agent that converts the hypo into harmless sodium sulfate.

Image plane Plane, normally at right angles to the lens axis, where a sharp image is formed. In photography, coincides with the film plane.

Incident light reading Measurement of light falling on a subject by a meter that faces the light source or camera position. Now an uncommon method of determining correct exposure.

Infinity Setting that places the lens as close as possible to the film plane, thus giving a sharp image of distant objects. On the focus ring, infinity is denoted by the symbol ∞.

Infrared Electromagnetic radiation with a wavelength longer than that of visible light – approximately 700 to 800 nanometers. Special film can record this radiation to produce a visible image. Infrared light does not focus in the same plane as visible light, thus requiring the lens focusing control to be adjusted.

Integral tripack Film or printing paper with three main emulsion layers inseparably coated on the same base, each sensitized to one of the primary colors of light. Almost all modern films are of this type. In addition to the three main emulsion layers, the tripack included a yellow filter below the blue-sensitive emulsion.

Interference Alteration of the wavelength of light resulting from the meeting of two wavefronts, as when light reflected from the back of a thin film meets light reaching the front.

Inverse square law A mathematic formula for calculating the increase or decrease in light intensity falling on a surface as the distance between the surface and a point source of light changes. The change of intensity is calculated by inversely squaring the change of distance. At twice the distance, the light is only one-quarter as intense. If the distance is reduced by three times the intensity of the light is increased nine times.

IR setting Special setting found on a lens focus control, often marked in red, used for infrared photography. Required because infrared radiations are focused further from the lens than visible light.

Iris diaphragm Aperture mechanism with adjustable metal leaves that form a circular opening in the middle.

Irradiation In photography, scattering of light through the film emulsion caused by multiple reflections from the minute silver halide crystals that make up the image.

ISO International Standards Organization – a universally accepted speed rating for film.

Joule Strictly speaking, a unit of measurement, equal to one watt-second, of the energy stored in an electronic flashgun for conversion into light. Used to indicate the output of light from an electronic flashgun.

Kelvin (K) Unit of temperature measurement, starting from absolute zero at -273°C, used to indicate the color balance of light. The higher the color temperature, the more blue-white subjects appear; lower color temperatures have a yellow-orange coloration.

Lamphouse Part of an enlarger containing the lamp or light source.

Latent image The invisible image stored in a photographic emulsion after exposure but before development. Light-struck silver halide grains in the emulsion change only at the atomic level and the job of the developer is to "amplify" those changes.

Lens Optical device for forming an image of an object, scene, or person by bending light rays reflected from the subject. Made of a transparent medium with at least one curved surface. Photographic lenses consist of numerous glass elements (each a lens) with different refractive indices, designed to correct all major aberrations.

Lens hood Shielding, usually funnel-shaped, designed to prevent stray light from outside the picture area reaching the lens and causing internal reflections. Lens hoods have different shapes to accommodate the varying angles of view of lenses with different focal lengths.

Local control Darkroom printing technique involving burning in or shielding (dodging) particular areas of the image area.

Long focus Refers to a lens with a focal length greater than the diagonal of the film format it covers.

Long Tom Colloquial term for a large, high-powered telephoto lens.

Low key Describes a picture composed mainly of dark, rich tones. Effect can be heightened by slight underexposure.

Lumen Unit of light intensity falling on a surface. A lumen-second refers to light of one lumen intensity for a duration of one second, or the equivalent, such as two lumens for half a second.

Macro lens Lens designed to resolve highest levels of detail at very close focusing distances, giving images up to life-size. Although not ideal, can also be used as a general photographic lens.

Macrophotography Photography with image scale from 1:1 (same size), up to approximately ten times magnification.

Magnification Relationship between the size of the object and a larger image formed by the lens on a camera or, in the darkroom, by an enlarger lens.

Masking In color reproduction, the technique of using negatives or positives made from the original and printing them in combination in order to alter tone, contrast, or color in the image. In its general sense, masking prevents light from reaching selected areas of the emulsion.

Mercury vapor lamp Enclosed arc lamp producing a bluish light generated by passing a current through a sealed tube filled with mercury vapor.

Micrometer Measurement of one millionth of a meter. The wavelengths of visible light are just below this measurement.

Microphotography Optical reduction of photographs to a microscopically small scale. The term is also sometimes used to mean the technique of photographing through microscopes. *See* Photomicrography.

Microprisms Small prisms molded into focusing screens, usually within a central circle, to assist focusing. The image appears discontinuous when out of focus.

Mired shift value Filter's ability to change the color quality of a light source, expressed as a plus or minus number of micro-reciprocal degrees. The mired value of a light source is found by dividing one million by its color temperature in degrees kelvin. Filters are assigned fixed mired shift values by which they will modify the mired value of a light source. Yellowish filters have positive mired shift values, which means that they raise the mired value of the light source and lower its color temperature. Bluish filters have negative values, lowering the mired value of a light source and raising its color temperature. A decamired is ten mireds – a color shift just detectable by the human eye.

Montage A composite picture made from several images, placed edge-to-edge or overlapping.

Motor drive Device for winding on the film and resetting the shutter by means of an electric motor. Two to four frames per second can be expected.

Nanometer (nm) One thousand millionth of a meter. A unit for measuring the wavelength of electromagnetic radiation.

Negative Image in which light areas of the subject are recorded as dark and, conversely, dark areas as light. In a color negative, subject colors are also recorded as their complementaries. During printing, these tones and colors are reversed again to produce a correct-looking image.

Negative carrier Holder for negatives and transparencies in an enlarger. Individual frames of film may be held by the edges between glass.

Negative lens A diverging lens, with at least one concave surface. In photography, normally used only in conjunction with converging lenses.

Newton's rings Colored rings appearing when two transparent surfaces are not quite in contact. This interference effect can be troublesome when negatives or slides are held between glass in the negative carrier of an enlarger.

Nodal point Intersection between the optical axis of a lens and an imaginary "principle plane of refraction" within a compound lens. This plane is near the front of the lens for incoming rays of light, and near the back of the lens for emerging rays. The rear nodal point is found on the plane where parallel light rays entering the lens would meet lines diverging from the point where they were brought into focus behind it. Focal length is the distance from the rear nodal point to the focal plane when the lens is set at infinity.

Opacity Describes a material's lack of transparency. An image transmitting half the light falling on it has an opacity of 2.

Open flash Non-automatic flash, fired manually between opening and closing the shutter. Flashguns incorporate an open flash button for testing or for use when the camera's shutter is held open using the B setting.

Optical axis Imaginary line through the center of an optical system running at right angles to the lenses and image plane.

Orthochromatic film Sensitive to the blue and green regions of the spectrum, but not to red or orange light.

Overdevelopment Excessive development, producing dense negatives of high contrast that will give featureless highlights when printed. Overdeveloped prints are fogged or stained.

Overexposure Excessive exposure, producing dense, flat negatives and pale transparencies with burned-out highlights. Overexposure in printing negatives produces darkened images.

Oxidation Chemical reaction relating to combination. Developers should be protected from oxidation by storing them in sealed bottles from which air has been expelled.

Pan-and-tilt head Tripod head with separate locks for horizontal (pan) and vertical (tilt) movements of the camera.

Panchromatic Describes emulsions that are sensitive to light of all colors.

Panning The action of swinging the camera while the shutter is open to follow a moving subject. Technique can produce a sharp image of the subject against a blurred background, thus providing an impression of movement. Degree of sharp detail and blurring depends on the shutter speed used and the speed of the swinging camera.

Panoramic camera Camera with a lens that travels in an arc during the exposure to make a record on a long strip of film that receives successive parts of a wide view. Once popular for large group pictures, such as school photographs.

Parallax error Difference between the image that is seen in a viewfinder and that which recorded by the taking lens. It is most pronounced at close distances with twin lens reflex (TLR) and direct-vision cameras. Single lens reflex(SLR) and studio cameras are free from parallax error.

Partitive color mixing The technique of placing

small areas of separate colors so close together that the eye combines them, making other colors. The photographs and diagrams in this book are produced using partitive color mixing.

Pentaprism Five-sided prism, which, in combination with the lens and mirror, can show an unreversed, upright image for eye-level viewing.

Perspective The relationship between objects in a scene in terms of scale, position, and shape when seen from one viewpoint. Because three-dimensional objects appear in this same perspective in a two-dimensional plane, such as a photograph, an impression of depth is created. The main elements of perspective in photography are diminishing size, converging lines, and overlapping forms, together with the recession of tone and color known as aerial perspective.

Photoelectric cell Light-sensitive cell that either generates electric current when light falls on it (as in a selenium cell) or reduces electrical resistance (as in a cadmium sulfide cell).

Photoflood Photographic lamp designed to be over-run in order to produce a high output of light during a comparatively short working life.

Photogrammetry The measurement of subjects such as buildings from photographs. Applies also to survey work and astronomy.

Photomicrography Photography that records magnified images of small or minute objects, generally by means of a camera attached to a microscope.

Physiogram Photographic recording of the pattern traced out by a point source of light attached to a complex moving pendulum.

Pincushion distortion Image distortion in which straight lines near the edge of the field appear to bend in the middle toward the lens axis.

Pinhole camera Camera that uses, instead of a lens, a small, sharp-edged hole in an opaque diaphragm. Requires very long exposures and gives indistinct and fuzzy images.

Plano-concave lens Lens with one flat side and the other concave. Similarly, a plano-convex lens has a flat side and a convex one. Used in the construction of compound lenses.

Plate Glass coated with light-sensitive emulsion. Once universally used, now available only for scientific purposes.

Plate camera Camera, usually of large format, originally intended for use with plates and now utilizing cut film.

Polarized light Light vibrating in one plane instead of in all directions at right angles around its line of motion. The polarization of specularly reflected light produces glare.

Polarizing filter Filter that passes on only polarized light and can be rotated to block polarized light reaching it, cutting down glare from polished surfaces or from blue sky.

Positive Print or transparency in which tones and colors correspond to those in the original subject.

Positive lens Converging or convex lens. Usually simple in construction.

Posterization Pictorial technique of tone separation in which a continuation range is split up into a few tones with intermediate detail suppressed.

Preservative Chemical, usually sodium sulfite, that preserves developing agents from oxidation while in solution by itself utilizing oxygen.

Primary colors Blue, green, and red, the regions of the spectrum that, in various combinations, can form any other color by additive mixing.

Prism Transparent medium, often of basic triangular shape, capable of bending, or refracting, light. Effect is to split "white" light into its component wavelengths into the colors of the visible spectrum.

Process lens Highly corrected lens used for copying illustrations for subsequent photomechanical reproduction. A process lens is normally a macro-type optic that covers a large format.

Pushing Prolonging development of film beyond the normally recommended duration in order to compensate for film underexposure or to increase contrast in the images.

Quartz-iodine lamp Incandescent lamp with a quartz envelope containing iodine.

R

Rack and pinion Mechanism for focusing used on many large-format cameras. The focusing wheel is fixed to a pinion wheel that engages in a toothed rack along the baseboard of the camera. When the wheel is turned the lens panel is slid along the baseboard.

Rangefinder Any device that measures the distance to an object using optical means. Now usually coupled to the focusing movements of the lens.

Reciprocity law States that the effect of exposure is equal to light intensity multiplied by duration. With extremely low intensities of light, or very high ones, this rule fails and extra exposure must be given in compensation. Very long exposures may have unpredictable results on color balance.

Reflected light reading A measurement of light reflected from the subject reaching the meter. Virtually all meters built into cameras utilize this principle of exposure measurement.

Reflector Surface capable of reflecting onto a subject light that is traveling away from it. White or gray cards are used in addition to metal reflectors.

Reflex camera Type of camera utilizing a mirror to reflect image-producing light rays from the taking lens onto a viewing screen for composition and focusing purposes.

Refraction The bending of light as it passes from one transparent medium to another of different density – a lens element, for example. The amount of bending a medium produces is described numerically by its refractive index.

Relative aperture Refers to the f numbers marked on lens barrels, and is obtained by dividing the focal length of a lens by the actual size of the aperture.

Resin-coated paper Printing paper treated with a synthetic resin to prevent the paper base from absorbing water or processing solutions. Results in shorter processing, washing, and drying times.

Resolution Ability of a lens and film to record adjacent fine detail.

Retina Light-sensitive area at the back of the eye containing specialized cells known as rods and cones. Light absorbed by these cells triggers electric signals for further analysis by a chain of cells leading to the cortex of the brain.

Reversal film *See* Color reversal film.

Reversing ring Ring that attaches to the camera body of an SLR, into which the lens is secured with the front element next to the body. The reversed lens allows greater image magnification and is used in close-up photography.

Ring flash Electronic flash arrangement that fits around the front of the lens and produces virtually shadowless lighting. Used in close-up photography.

Rising front Lens arrangement that can be moved vertically so that the lens rises above, or drops below, its normal position. Invaluable in architectural photography to prevent distortion of verticals in tall buildings when the camera is tilted so that the film plane is no longer parallel with the subject.

Rods Light-sensitive cells in the retina of the eye responsible for vision at low light levels. The rods are sensitive to light at low intensities but do not discriminate colors.

S

Sandwiching The projection or printing of two or more negatives or slides together to produce a composite image.

Saturated color Pure spectral color reflecting light of only one or two of the three main areas of the spectrum with no admixture of the third, which would have the effect of desaturating the hue toward white, gray, or black.

Secondary colors Colors resulting from mixing together any two of the primary colors – red, green, or blue. The principal secondary colors used in color film and printing processes are cyan (blue-green), magenta (red-blue), and yellow (red-green).

Shades Hues with a mixture of black.

Shutter Mechanical device used to expose film to light for an exact period of time. Between-the-lens leaf and focal plane shutters are the two main types used in cameras.

Silhouette Recording of a subject basically in terms of its shape. Usually achieved through backlighting or by illuminating a background while preventing light from falling on the subject.

Silver halides Generic name for light-sensitive compounds of silver with a halogen (iodine, bromine, chlorine, fluorine). Silver bromide is the main constituent of photographic emulsions, but silver iodide and silver chloride are also used. The latent image produced on these compounds by the action of light can be converted to metallic silver by the action of developers.

Single lens reflex (SLR) Camera system utilizing a hinged mirror between the lens and the film, which swings out of the light path when the shutter is open, allowing the taking function of the lens to substitute for the viewing function of the lens.

Slave unit Photoelectric device, which, when activated by light from the main flash, fires one or more auxiliary flashes.

SLR *See* Single lens reflex.

Snoot Attachment (often tubular) for lamp reflectors or spotlights used to control the spread of light.

Soft-focus image Photographic image that is not critically sharp. Any lens that is incapable of pin-sharp definition will produce this effect, or a soft-focus attachment can be added to the front of a lens.

Spectrum Range of colors in the visible part of electromagnetic radiation that can be produced by dispersion or diffraction. The spectrum is customarily divided into regions of red, orange, yellow, green, blue, indigo, and violet. The wavelength band ranges from violet at about 380nm to red at700nm.

Specular reflection Reflection of light rays from a smooth surface at the same angle. The slight unevenness of most surfaces normally produces diffuse reflection with rays bouncing off in all directions.

Spherical aberration Inability of a lens to bring light passing through its edge to the same point of focus as light passing through its center. Controlled spherical aberration is used in soft-focus lenses and attachments.

Spot meter Exposure meter that measures reflected light from a small area of the subject or scene. Used for high-contrast subjects.

Standard lens Lens with a focal length approximately equal to the diagonal of the camera's film format.

Stopping down Decreasing the lens aperture to control exposure or increase depth of field.

Subtractive color process Means of producing a color image by using filters or dyes to absorb some primary components of light, allowing only others to form the image. The subtractive primaries used in most color reproduction processes are cyan (blocking red), magenta (blocking green), and yellow (blocking blue).

Synchronized flash Flash automatically fired at the moment when the shutter is fully open so that all of the film area receives flash light reflected back toward the camera from the subject.

T

Telephoto lens Compact type of lens with a focal length greater than the diagonal of the film format it covers.

Test strip Strip of printing paper that receives several different exposures, section by section, from the same film image so that (after the strip is developed) exposure and filtration can be judged before making an enlargement.

Tint Color that has been made lighter by the addition of white.

TLR *See* Twin lens reflex.

Tonal range Range of tones between the lightest and darkest areas, usually of a positive image.

Transmitted light Light that has passed through a transparent or translucent medium, as opposed to light that has been reflected by an opaque surface.

T setting Time setting – device fitted to some shutter mechanisms that allows the shutter to open when the release is depressed, and to remain open until the release is depressed a second time. Used for long, manually timed exposures.

TTL (through the lens) Metering system that uses cells inside the camera body that react only to the light transmitted by the camera lens. Most modern SLR cameras have this type of metering.

Tungsten-halogen lamp Incandescent lamp with a tungsten filament and a halogen (iodine and/or bromine) contained in a sealed glass or quartz envelope. The halogen prevents the glass blackening.

Twin lens reflex (TLR) Camera system with separate, but identical, viewing and taking lenses. The upper (viewing) lens has a mirror behind it that reflects light to a focusing screen held at waist level, which displays a laterally reversed image of the scene or subject.

U

Ultraviolet (UV) light Invisible electromagnetic radiation of a shorter wavelength than blue light. Photographic materials are sensitive to this radiation, which, on hazy days, can increase aerial perspective unless counteracted by an ultraviolet filter.

Uprating Rating of a film at a higher speed index than normal. In practical terms, it means underexposing. For example, uprating an ISO 400 film to ISO 800 represents a one-stop underexposure and this is usually compensated for by increasing development time.

V

View camera Large-format camera with main camera movements. Usually takes single-sheet cut film. Also known as a field or technical camera.

Viewfinder Screen built into a camera, or a separate, simple frame, by means of which the photographer can see the field of view of the lens. Most viewfinders incorporate a focusing system.

Viewpoint Relationship between camera position and subject when a photograph is taken. Viewpoint is the primary factor in determining the perspective of a photograph.

W

Wavelength Distance between successive similar points on an alternating wave. Inversely proportional to the frequency of the radiation.

Working solution Processing solution at a strength suitable for use without being further diluted, as opposed to a concentrated stock solution.

Index

Acknowledgments

The author and publisher would like to thank the following people and organizations for their help in the preparation of this book:
Jon Richardson at Kodak; Pam Walker at Kyocera Yashica; John Dickins at Pentax; and David Ballantine at Hasselblad. Thanks also go to Michael Dyer Associates, the Carter family, Icelandic Tourist Board, Guernsey Tourist Board, Ironbridge Gorge, Greenwich Royal Naval College, Austrian Tourist Board, Westminster Abbey, Daisy and Rose Peasgood, Jenny Mackintosh, Julia North, and Elaine Winkworth.

Apart from photographs of equipment, all pictures in this book were taken by John Hedgecoe.